Empire of the Inca

BARBARA A. SOMERVILL

Facts On File, Inc.

Great Empires of the Past: EMPIRE OF THE INCA

HISTORY CONSULTANT: Lucy C. Salazar, Ph.D., archaeologist and curatorial affiliate in anthropology at Yale University's Peabody Museum; project manager for Machu Picchu.

Facts On File, Inc.
132 West 31st Street
New York NY 10001

Library of Congress Cataloging-in-Publication Data
Somervill, Barbara A.
Empire of the Inca / Barbara Somervill.
p. cm. – (Great empires of the past)
Includes bibliographical references and index.
ISBN 0-8160-5560-2 (hc: alk. paper)
1. Incas–History. 2. Incas–Social life and customs. I. Title.
II. Series.
F3429.S66 2004
985' .019–dc22   2004003952

Facts On File books are available at special discounts when purchased in bulk quantities for businesses, associations, institutions, or sales promotions. Please call our Special Sales Department in New York at (212) 967-8800 or (800) 322-8755.

You can find Facts On File on the World Wide Web at http://www.factsonfile.com

Produced by the Shoreline Publishing Group LLC
Editorial Director: James Buckley Jr.
Series Editor: Beth Adelman
Designed by Thomas Carling, Carling Design, Inc.
Photo research by Julie Chung, PhotoSearch, Inc., New York
Index by Word Co.

Photo and art credits: Jeremy Horner/Corbis: 1, 76; John Mair, Jr./Image Works: 3, 99; AP/Wide World Photos: 4, 85, 88, 118; Fair Street Pictures: 10, 14, 38, 44; Brooklyn Museum of Art, New York/Bridgeman Art Library: 12; Charles Walker/Topfoto/Image Works: 17; Mark Godfrey/Image Works: 20; Wolfgang Kaehler/Corbis: 21; Hubert Stadler/Corbis: 26; Facts on File: 32, 115; Ryan Fox/Lonely Planet Images: 34; Stock Montage, Inc.: 40; Courtesy Department Library Services American Museum of Natural History, Neg. No. 286821: 47; Bildarchiv Preussischer Kulturbesitz/Art Resource, NY: 50; Charles & Josette Lenars/Corbis: 55; Museum of Fine Arts, Houston, Texas/Bridgeman Art Library: 60; Werner Forman/Art Resource, NY: 68; Nick Sanders/Barbara Heller Photo Library, London/Art Resource, NY: 71; Tony Savino/Image Works: 74; Courtesy of the American Museum of Natural, Neg. 2A 3174: 82; Bibliothèque des Artes Decoratifs, Paris, France/Bridgeman Art Library: 90; Katie Attenborough/Bridgeman Art Library: 92, 105; SEF/Art Resource, NY: 96; Anthony Pidgeon/Lonely Planet Images: 110; Mark Daffey/Lonely Planet Images: 113

Printed in the United States of America

VB PKG 10 9 8 7 6 5 4 3 2 1

This book is printed on acid-free paper.

CONTENTS

Introduction

UNCOVERING FACTUAL DATA ABOUT THE INCA EMPIRE requires a formidable team of experts: mathematicians, archaeologists, and historians. Mathematicians work to unravel the only concrete records left by people of the empire—*quipus*, knotted strings that tabulated the Inca population and productivity down to the last dehydrated potato. Archaeologists dig up ancient temples, buried cities, and shrouded mummies that tell of a complex society. Historians delve into the chronicles of Spanish conquistadors, priests, and government clerks—the only written records of the Inca culture. And all must separate fact from fiction, dealing with a culture whose history is intertwined with legends of stone warriors and visits from the gods.

The task is made more difficult because the Inca Empire had no written language—not even hieroglyphs or pictograms—or numerical system. The Inca civilization passed its history along by means of oral tradition. Thus, the founding of the empire may have taken place in 1200—or not. Dates and details of the early Inca Empire are all estimates.

The initial arrival of the Spanish in 1524 and their mania for cataloguing even their smallest accomplishments produced the first concrete records of Inca life. Thus, the early period from 1200 to about 1525 presents a blend of fact and fiction, legends and daring deeds, mingled with cultural pride. Historians have been frustrated in their pursuit of accuracy because there is simply no way to separate tales of greatness from feats of greatness.

Even the term *inca* adds confusion to studying the empire. The word *inca* refers to a single person, a social class, and a civilization—and is applied with little discrimination as to the term's true meaning. *Inca* is a

OPPOSITE
Machu Picchu
High on a mountaintop in the Andes, 310 miles southeast of Lima, Peru, the ruins of Machu Picchu are a testament to the talents of Inca builders.

5

Quechua word that means "leader" or "chief." The empire's supreme leader, a kind of king or emperor, bore the title *inca* or *sapa inca* (unique leader or chief). Thirteen sapa incas ruled the empire with varying degrees of success. Although there were sapa incas after Atahuallpa, such as Manco Inca and Tupac Amaru, they had no power. Once the Spanish took over, they controlled the land and people–and the sapa inca.

The sapa inca led a noble class that numbered about 1,000 men. These nobles were called *incas* or *capac incas*, and they served as government, religious, and military leaders of the empire, as well as being directly related to the sapa inca. Women played leadership roles in some areas of life, especially those that involved other women, but they were generally not leaders of groups that included men.

Today, people often refer to all citizens living under the rule of the Incas as "Incas;" they were not. They were conquered cultures and civilizations absorbed into the empire. Consider the history of the Roman Empire and their many conquests. Falling under Roman rule did not make the Greek or Egyptian people Romans, simply Roman subjects accountable to their Roman prefects. The same was true of conquered people living under the Incas. Inca subjects often continued to worship their own gods, as long as they also paid homage to the primary Inca gods: the sun, the moon, and thunder-lightning. They wore their ethnic style of clothing, and empire administrators actually prohibited subjects from wearing the clothes or headgear of any other ethnic group or region.

The empire began in Cuzco, a village founded by Manco Capac, the first sapa inca, and settled by his followers. The village still exists in what is today southeastern Peru. Eventually, Inca influence spread from the eastern foothills of the Andes Mountains to the Pacific Ocean, from present-day Ecuador in the north to modern Chile and Argentina in the south. The sapa inca ruled over land that stretched 2,500 miles along western South America, or roughly the distance from Los Angeles, California to Charleston, South Carolina. Again, this is an educated estimate, since no records, detailed maps, or exact borders exist from those times.

The empire did not arise as a new civilization with innovative concepts of religion, agriculture, arts, music, or warfare. Instead, it assimilated other cultures, absorbed people into its vast labor force, and instilled Inca values and beliefs into those living within the realm. At the same time, the empire welcomed new ideas and, after experimentation, improved on accepted modes of artistic expression and technology. For example, the Inca Empire is noted for its brilliant use of stone architecture. Advanced

WHAT ARE CONNECTIONS?

Throughout this book, and all the books in the Great Empires of the Past series, you will find Connections boxes. They point out ideas, inventions, art, food, customs, and more from this empire that are still part of our world today.

Nations and cultures in remote history can seem far removed from our world, but these connections demonstrate how our everyday lives have been shaped by the peoples of the past.

masonry techniques were not the original invention of the Incas, but were inspired by the work of the conquered Tiahuanaco culture that lived near Lake Titicaca. While the Incas improved upon and adapted these techniques, they owe much to the Tiahuanaco. Museum-quality gold and silver metalwork came from exploiting vanquished Chimu artisans.

The *Cronistas*

Much of what we know today about the Inca Empire comes to us from Spanish *cronistas*, soldiers, clerks and clerics who wrote detailed accounts of the history, customs, and daily lives of Inca citizens. Some (but not all) of the Spanish who came to the Inca realm were highly literate and many kept journals, wrote letters, and recorded the events of their conquest. *Cronistas* provide primary source material from the viewpoint of a conquering people who came from a very different cultural background.

The 13 Sapa Incas

There are no exact birth and death dates for these leaders, except for the deaths of the last five. Instead, we have provided the estimated dates of when they ruled.

Manco Capac, ruled c. 1200

Sinchi Roca, ruled c. 1228–1258

Lloque Yupanqui, ruled c. 1258–1288

Mayta Capac, ruled c. 1288–1318

Capac Yupanqui, ruled c. 1318–1348

Inca Roca ruled, c. 1348–1378

Yahuar Huacac, ruled c. 1378–1408

Huiracocha, ruled c. 1408–1438

Pachacuti (Cusi Yupanqui), ruled 1438–1471

Tupac Yupanqui, ruled 1471–1493

Huayna Capac, ruled 1493–1525

Huáscar, ruled 1525–1532

Atahuallpa, ruled 1532–1533

Felipe Guaman Poma de Ayala (c. 1538–c. 1620), an Andes native, wrote the longest and perhaps most valuable document about the Inca Empire, *La nueva crónica y buen gobierno* (the new chronicle and good government). This 1,179-page manuscript contains accounts of Inca culture, history, occupations, religious practices, and civil government. Guaman Poma included more than 400 drawings with his writing (some of them are reproduced throughout this book, starting on page 10). Although written in the early 1600s, Guaman Poma's manuscript was not discovered until 1908, when German scholar Richard Pietschmann found the document in the archives of the Royal Danish Library in Copenhagen.

Garcilaso de la Vega (1539–1616) was the son of the Spanish conquistador Sebastian de la Vega Vargas and the Inca princess Chimpu

Ocllo. Garcilaso combined a classic European-style education with knowledge of and empathy for the Inca culture. His writings about the Inca civilization are detailed, picturesque, and engaging. They span several volumes grouped under the title *The Incas: Royal Commentaries*. The Royal Council of Madrid was not enthusiastic about Garcilaso de la Vega's chronicle, so they changed the title from *Royal Commentaries* to *General History of Peru*.

Scholars know very little about Juan de Betanzos (c. 1550), author of *Suma y narracíon de los Inca* (narrative of the Incas). He was Spanish by birth but lived in Peru most of his life. Betanzos may have been a Spanish scribe or a government clerk, as well as an interpreter who investigated native traditions and customs. He married an Inca woman, lived in Cuzco in the 1540s, and was fluent in Spanish and Quechua (the language of the Incas), which Spanish *corregidors* (royal administrators) found useful. His Narrative of the Incas has been translated into English and provides one of the earliest accounts of Inca culture.

Cronista Pedro de Cieza de León (c. 1518–1560) was Spanish born and educated and traveled through much of the Inca realm as a soldier. His *Crónica del Peru* (chronicle of Peru), published in 1553, presents richly detailed accounts of the Spanish conquest from a military viewpoint. He provides accurate geographical descriptions of the region and explanations of the Inca government and culture. He also explains the strategy used by the relatively small Spanish conquering forces in defeating the Incas.

Cieza de León observed the Inca people and had an uncanny understanding of their ways. This is how he described the Inca work ethic in his *Crónica*: "No one who was lazy or tried to live by the work of others was tolerated; everyone had to work. Thus on certain days each lord went to his lands and took the plow in hand and cultivated the earth, and did other things. Even the Incas themselves did this to set an example. And under their system, there was none such in all the kingdom, for, if he had his health, he worked and lacked for nothing; and if he was ill, he received what he needed from the storehouses."

CONNECTIONS >>>>>>>>>>>>>

Do You Speak Quechua?

Some Quechua words have found their way into the English language. These include coca, condor, guano (bat or bird manure, used for fertilizer), lima (as in the bean), llama, puma, quinine, quinoa (a type of grain), and vicuña (an Andean animal that is related to the llama; the word also means the cloth made from wool from that animal).

Soldiers marveled at the technology and wealth of the Incas, but Roman Catholic priests saw only "pagan" rites and "heathen" idols. The goal of the Catholic clergy in Peru was to convert the native people to Christianity. Eradication of Native worship took precedence as priests reduced Inca sacred idols and temples to rubble and replaced the culture's heritage with their own. The Spanish clergy met with mixed success; the Native population concealed the locations of many sacred Inca sites and icons and mingled their traditional polytheism (worship of more than one god) with Roman Catholic practices.

Father Bernabé Cobo (1582–1657), a Jesuit priest and missionary, wrote the least biased, most accurate account of Inca history by a priest in his book *Historia del Nuevo Mundo* (the history of the new world). He arrived in Peru in 1599 to embark on a missionary career and traveled extensively throughout Peru and northern Bolivia. Cobo was basically an early historian, and most of his writings were based on library research using the work of earlier Spanish *cronistas*, as well as some personal observations and oral information, yet Cobo compiled an extensive and convincing catalog of the Inca Empire.

In addition to the Spanish accounts, a few Native Andean chroniclers wrote histories of the Incas. These chroniclers wrote much later than the Spanish. The best known of these was Juan de Santa Cruz Pachacutiyamqui Salcamayhua, who wrote a history of Peru in the early 17th century. Another prolific Native historian was Inca Diego del Castro Titu Cusi Yupanqui. Titu Cusi wrote 22 volumes on the history of the Incas and their conquest by the Spanish. Using both Spanish and Native American resources provides a balanced view of Inca history.

The Inca Legacy

If the *cronistas* could enumerate the lessons to be learned from the Inca Empire, their lists would be lengthy. They might note that the civilization thrived despite lacking a written language, a number system, and one of humanity's greatest inventions–the wheel.

Despite these obvious handicaps, the Inca Empire developed and administered a socialist type government in which it was rare to find a citizen who was hungry, naked, or homeless. Under Inca rule, the sick were generally well-cared for and the elderly could expect to receive tender consideration. All this occurred without corruption in a society that was relatively crime-free. No modern government has provided so completely for its citizens.

The Sapa Inca
This picture of the sapa inca in his litter is one of Felipe Guaman Poma de Ayala's drawings from La nueva crónica y buen gobierno *(the new chronicle and good government). Accounts such as Ayala's are one of the main ways we know about the Incas.*

Although difficult to decipher, the Inca method of record keeping with strings and knots—the *quipu*—proved as effective (if not more so) than today's powerful computers when it came to population and productivity statistics. Every region, every farm, and every single taxpayer appeared in the *quipus*. The Incas accepted no plus-or-minus variables.

Inca building technology offers lessons many countries would find valuable today. Inca masons built walls of stone in which the face of the wall is designed to fit so tightly that the mortar is hidden; these walls have held up over many centuries and countless earthquakes. Engineers constructed irrigation ditches, canals, and aqueducts that provided fresh water and sanitation to cities at a time when European towns had open sewers that spread disease among the population. Paved roads ran up the Andes Mountains, along cliff edges, over deserts, and through jungles—and many of those roads still exist today. Where needed, bridges spanned chasms hundreds of feet deep and lasted more than 100 years, despite being built of reeds, leather, and logs. By 1500, the planned city of Cuzco had more than 4,000 stone buildings, complete with sparkling fountains, rock-lined sewers, and sprawling public plazas.

The empire combined diverse cultures into one civilization ruled by a single man, the sapa inca. Throughout the realm, all citizens were required to learn Quechua, the language of the Incas. Subjects followed the same laws and suffered the same punishments for illegal acts—which were surprisingly few, since the punishment for most crimes was death.

A bureaucratic network of administrators, record keepers, and government spies kept the government running smoothly, and corruption, jealousy, and ambition were not common among Inca leaders. From cradle to grave, most Inca subjects accepted their roles in life and the laws that governed them: Do not be lazy, steal, lie, commit adultery, or murder. The Inca civilization thrived under a simple philosophy: Work hard, pay tax, and want for nothing.

PART I

HISTORY

The Beginning of the Empire

The Empire at Its Greatest

The Final Years of Inca Rule

CHAPTER 1

The Beginning of the Empire

MANY LEGENDS TELL OF HOW THE FIRST INCA, MANCO CAPAC, and his wife, Mama Ocllo, established the Inca Empire. The legends are imaginative, creative, and compelling, and represent the foundations of Peru's cultural heritage and oral tradition dating back 800 years.

One legend tells of four brothers: Ayar Cachi, Ayar Uchu, Ayar Auca, and Ayar Manco. The family lived in the cavern of Pacaritambo, a deep cave cut into the Andes Mountains. The four brothers and their four sisters left their home in search of a better existence. The first brother, Ayar Cachi, had mystical powers greatly coveted by the other siblings. The jealous brothers tricked Ayar Cachi into returning to their cave, which they blocked with stones to prevent Ayar Cachi from escaping.

The remaining three came upon Mount Huanacauri during their journey. When they reached the mountain, Uchu turned to stone and became a holy shrine, or huaca, revered by the Inca people. This left only Ayar Auca and Ayar Manco, who walked to a small village where Ayar Auca became frightened and fled. He scrambled across the rough terrain until exhaustion overcame him; then he sat down to rest and, like his brother, was turned to stone.

Ayar Manco traveled on with his sisters, finally arriving at a place between the Urubamba and Apurímac Rivers. There, Ayar Manco founded the city of Cuzco and the culture that would later become the Inca Empire. Manco selected his sister Mama Ocllo as his wife because she had a complacent and gracious personality. The marriage accounts for the Inca custom of a sapa inca usually marrying his full-blooded sister. Ayar Manco changed his name to Manco Capac and proclaimed himself ruler over the new society. Later, the title of sapa inca was most often passed to a son of

OPPOSITE

Founding Ruler
Manco Capac, the first sapa inca, is shown here in an 18th century Peruvian oil painting.

13

the primary wife, the *coya*. The crown did not always go to the firstborn son, but whichever son of the *coya* seemed best suited to become the emperor.

Another version of the Inca Empire's beginning involves the sun god Inti, Manco Capac, and Mama Ocllo. The tale begins as members of 10 familial clans (*ayllus*) follow Manco Capac on his journey. Along the way, the sun god gives Manco Capac a golden rod, commanding him to plunge the rod into the earth when Manco arrives at a suitable location for settlement. Supposedly, Manco followed this advice on a high plain in the Andes, the rod disappeared, and the leader and his community founded Cuzco at the selected site. Manco Capac then built a temple, the Intihuasi, to honor the sun on the exact spot where the golden rod disappeared into the earth.

The legends have been passed down from father to son, mother to daughter. Historians accept that Manco Capac was the founding father and the first inca, or chief, of a clan of people who lived in the Andes. The city of Cuzco stands today as a testament to the empire's existence. Exact details of when and how the empire began remain shrouded in mystery.

Equally mysterious are the many civilizations that thrived in the Andes and the surrounding regions before the Incas came to power. These civilizations contribute to the Inca story because they fostered the art, culture, political organization, and religious beliefs of the Inca Empire. The names given to these cultures are not nec-

14

essarily what the people called themselves, because archaeologists designate culture names for the locations where ruins of their civilizations have been found. So, for example, the Moche culture was a group that once lived in the Moche Valley in northern Peru.

Pre-Columbian (before Christopher Columbus arrived in the Americas) civilizations are recognized as cultures or horizons. A culture defines the beliefs, society, art, and lifestyle of a contained group. A horizon indicates cultural beliefs, art, and lifestyles spread over a large region and a number of diverse ethnic groups.

The early cultures that most influenced the Incas include the Chavín horizon, and the Moche, Paracas, Nazca, and Tiahuanaco cultures. These groups existed before Manco Capac founded the Inca Empire, and their artifacts and technology were evaluated and incorporated into the Inca culture. None of these cultures had a written language, so dates and details of each group have been estimated by carbon-dating methods.

The Chavín Horizon

From 900 to 200 B.C.E., the people of Chavín thrived in the eastern *cordillera* (mountain range) of present-day Peru. They controlled trade between the Pacific Ocean and the Amazon River region because of their pivotal location along well-traveled mountain passes. Chavín art, beliefs, and social customs spread throughout the Andes through human contact and llama caravans that were packed with Chavín pottery, cloth, and metalwork.

This culture believed in the close link between the human and animal worlds and that it was possible to move between them in the mythical and the ritual world. They made icons with anthropomorphized animals

(animals with human forms or personality), including eagles, falcons, and snakes. Cats posed as humans appear on ceramic drinking vessels, urns, plates, and on murals in temples.

In textiles, the Chavín developed the use of llama and alpaca wool in weaving. They advanced the use of natural dyes and cloth painting, as well as hand-spinning yarn and weaving on back-braced looms. These techniques became standard among the Chavín and spread among other cultures through trade. By the time the Inca Empire began, Chavín weaving techniques had become the yardstick for quality textiles.

Fly With the Nazca?

A Nazca legend tells of Antarqui, a boy who helped the Incas during battles by flying overhead and reporting on enemy soldiers and their locations. Nazca ceramic artifacts portray flying people. In addition, cloth has been found in tombs that has such a tight weave that the cloth could hold air. When tested by a hot air balloon manufacturer, the cloth was shown to have a tighter weave than that company used for making modern hot air balloons. Could the Nazca possibly have had the technology to fly?

Peter James and Nick Thorpe, in their book *Ancient Inventions,* suggest they may have, based on an archaeological experiment done by the Explorers Society:

> The Society tested the feasibility of Nazca ballooning by construction of their own balloon, which they named *Condor I.* It was made from cotton and wood, with a gondola of reeds from Lake Titicaca to hold the passengers. The balloon was to be filled with hot smoke produced from burning extremely dry wood....
>
> On November 23, 1975, American Jim Woodman of the Explorers Society and English balloonist Julian Nott ascended to 380 feet in *Condor I,* stayed in the air for several minutes and then descended again safely, thus completing a remarkable piece of experimental archaeology. Of course this does not prove that the ancient Nazcans did fly, but it certainly shows that it is a very real possibility.

The Paracas Culture

Most of what is known today about the Paracas culture that began in about 600 B.C.E. comes from studying the Paracas cemetery in southern Peru, not far from the city of Ica. In this city of the dead, bodies were buried in a crouching position. The corpses were wrapped in cloth and placed in large baskets. Due to the exceptionally dry conditions, the bodies were naturally mummified. Many bodies were wrapped in finely embroidered cotton or wool, with designs of mythical creatures, animals, and geometric patterns. The condition of each mummified body tells much about the culture. Skulls were flattened, a result of binding infants' heads at birth. Many Native American cultures considered a flat skull to be a sign of beauty, and the condition of Paracas skulls gives anthropologists an insight into the cultural beliefs of the Paracas people.

Along with the bodies, archaeologists found weapons, gold

jewelry and ornaments, feather fans, petrified animals, pottery, and gourds. The artifacts provide information about burial practices, technology, and art of the Paracas. Scientists know that the Paracas had technology for weaving cloth, metalwork, and ceramics. They infer that the culture believed in an afterlife in which the deceased would need weapons, food, and personal effects.

The Nazca Culture

Around 200 C.E., the Paracas culture gave way to the Nazca civilization. The Nazca people were artists and craftspeople who produced highly polished, decorated ceramics, and embroidered intricate designs into wool and cotton cloth. The Nazca culture also produced remarkable rock patterns on the sandy desert soil. These patterns can only be seen from the air, which makes their construction even more astounding. The stone patterns represent birds, crabs, and flowers. One bird measures 400 feet by 300 feet. The edges of the designs point to the four main points of the compass.

Weaving skills among the Nazca were one of the culture's most remarkable talents. As with the Chavín, Nazca textile technology was passed from mother to daughter over many generations. By the time the Inca Empire emerged, the textile technology of both early cultures had permeated the practices of spinning, dyeing, and weaving throughout the Andes.

How Did They Do That?
This Nazca image of a monkey is traced in the sandy desert soil, and is so big that it is visible only from the air.

The Moche Culture

In the Moche and Chicama valleys of Peru, a civilization emerged that lasted roughly 600 years. They are called the Moche culture, a clan that thrived from about 100 to 700. The Moche developed a dominant noble class that included priests and military leaders. They founded the first kingdom of the Andes and united weaker cultures under their king.

Like other early civilizations in the Americas, the Moche had no written language. However, archaeologists have discovered much about the Moche people's beliefs and practices through their art. The Moche legacy lives in the ceramics of the culture. Pictures on bowls, jars, urns, and plates portray the Moche people in every aspect of life. Moche doctors perform brain surgery and set broken bones. Weavers spin and work their looms. Messengers carry important news along Moche roads while ancient soldiers wield their slings and lances to protect their kingdom. Moche pottery also depicts food, boats, houses, and farming practices, along with common animals, such as llamas, pumas, frogs, and birds.

Moche construction technology was advanced for its time. The culture produced many large buildings, principally made of adobe. At Cerro Blanco in Peru, pyramids stand as a reminder of the Moche culture. The Huaca del Sol (Shrine of the Sun) and the Huaca de la Luna (Shrine of the Moon) were massive temples made of adobe blocks and built on sprawling temple platforms. The Huaca de la Luna's base measures 750 feet by 450 feet. These structures existed when the Incas conquered the people living in the Moche Valley about 600 years after the Moche civilization had disappeared. The ability to make adobe bricks that lasted must have impressed Inca architects. Although later Inca architecture used cut stone, early works and peasant dwellings in certain regions used straw-and-mud adobe bricks.

Because the Moche Valley lay in the dry desert of northern Peru, the culture developed advanced agricultural techniques. They used guano (sea bird droppings) and livestock manure to fertilize their fields, and they built earthen aqueducts to carry water for irrigation and for human use. These techniques were still in use when the Inca Empire began. The Incas were quick to recognize the value of Moche agricultural technology to produce more food for their ever-growing empire. The use of irrigation and fertilizers reached its height during Inca days, but the original concept came from the Moche culture.

The Tiahuanaco Culture

On the southern shore of Lake Titicaca, in present-day Bolivia, the Tiahuanaco civilization thrived during the first millennium. Dates for the Tiahuanaco vary; some archaeologists believe the Tiahuanaco culture emerged in 100, and others think it was closer to 200. The disappearance of the culture is also in dispute, and estimates range from 600 to 1250, with 1150 the most likely time.

The significance of the Tiahuanaco people depends less on when they existed and more on what they accomplished. This was a culture of architects, masons, and advanced building technology. No early South

A FARMER'S ALMANAC

The Tiahuanacos made a temple entrance called the Gateway to the Sun out of one single, huge stone. Ornately carved and precisely hewn, the gateway reaches 12 feet high and weighs an estimated 10 tons. The relief carvings on the Gateway of the Sun represent condors, tigers, and serpents. Some historians believe the Gateway was a pictorial calendar that marked the winter and summer solstice and the spring and fall equinox. The calendar may also have been a work schedule, marking when to plant, weed, water, and harvest. Modern farmers plan their work according to the same seasonal changes marked by the Tiahuanacos in their massive stone calendar.

American cultures developed the wheel, yet these ancient people built massive stone temples, courts, and cities. The Tiahuanaco developed masonry to such a high degree that they could erect large stone buildings where the blocks fit together so well that the mortar between them is almost invisible. They carved stones to fit one inside the next by means of insets, copper clamps, and tenons (carved joints).

By the time the Incas encountered the Tiahuanacos, their civilization had collapsed. But knowledge of their building techniques has been retained and was later absorbed by the Incas. Before Inca expansion, the Incas did build stone buildings, but much coarser ones than in classic Inca times. The master masons brought from Lake Titicaca played a role in improving the quality of stonework created by the Inca state.

The First Incas

The Inca Empire began with a small group of people who lived in crude homes and scrambled for food. They spent their earliest years defending their territory from invading enemy tribes and trying to eke out enough crops to last through droughts and famines. The first eight Inca rulers focused on Cuzco and its surrounding towns. In the early days, the Inca civilization consisted of a population of well under 10,000 people, and Cuzco under Manco Capac probably only had 500 residents.

The early history of the Incas is bound up with myths that are difficult to separate from facts. Recounting this history is made all the more difficult because the Incas had no written language, and oral history can sometimes change with the retelling. Still, there is a story of how the Inca civilization began.

Manco Capac and Mama Ocllo brought together the small tribes living near Cuzco. The tribes formed *ayllus* (clans) under the guidance of Manco Capac, the first Inca ruler. The *ayllu* system endured throughout the 300-year reign of imperial rule. Setting up a new city demanded constant attention and ensuring that the people had the basic elements of life: food, clothing, and shelter. The Incas had to build housing, till fields and plant crops, hunt, and find potable water. Manco Capac also built a sun temple, Intihuasi, so that the people of Cuzco could honor their primary god.

Blending the four tribes around Cuzco together was not difficult. The members of these tribes were farmers who had no interest in war. However, neighboring tribes were not as friendly. A significant achievement of Manco Capac's reign was to provide a safe, secure home for his people and an heir to provide continuous leadership.

Sinchi Roca, Manco Capac's heir, ruled from roughly 1228 to 1258. Among his first duties was to build a palace for himself and his family, servants, and guards. Each succeeding Inca chief needed to build a new home, as the mummified remains of earlier Inca rulers continued to reside in their original palaces, along with their families and servants.

Improvements needed to be made to the Intihuasi since the original, according to Spanish priest Bernabé Cobo, was "of humble and coarse adobe walls . . . because in those rustic times the people did not have a way to work stone as their descendants did later." The temple served a dual purpose for the Incas, providing a place to worship and intimidating people of neighboring tribes, who were awed by the size of the temple. This was particularly true of civilizations that had no formal places of worship.

Cuzco's location high in the Andes had a short growing season and a long winter. The growing population needed more food, and the responsibility to ensure higher crop yields fell to the Inca ruler. Sinchi Roca settled on two ideas that would help increase farmland: building agricultural terraces and draining the local marsh. Each of these projects consumed millions of hours of labor. Humans and llamas carried innumerable stones to form the terraced walls. Filling the terraces required thousands of baskets of topsoil, which then needed to be raked, seeded, weeded, and watered. Draining marshland was even more difficult, since sloped channels needed to be cut into the earth using rudimentary tools.

The foresight of Sinchi Rocha meant that his son, Lloque Yupanqui, the third Inca chief, did not face additional agricultural demands. Instead, his main accom-

Weaving History
Weaving is still important in the Andes, and weavers still use a backstrap loom, as the Incas did. The strap at the bottom of the loom is secured around the weaver's waist to keep it stable.

CONNECTIONS >>>>>>>>>>>>>>>>>>>>>>>>>>>>>>>>>

Open Markets Endure

Lloque Yupanqui's open markets were much like farmer's markets of today. Farmers brought surplus crops, such as potatoes, corn, and quinoa (a type of grain) to trade with other vendors who offered cloth, leather goods, pottery, and dried and smoked meat or fish. The Incas did not have any currency, so all purchases were bartered for goods based on values set by buyer and seller. Three such markets existed in Cuzco, and the tradition continues to this day.

Today, market day in Andes towns brings a flurry of activity, as vendors set up stalls and buyers compare produce and goods on offer. Surprisingly, many of the products remain the same: woven cloth, leather goods, dried meat or fish, corn, potatoes, medicinal and cooking herbs, and pottery. Buyers can make purchases in cash now, although the barter system still enables vendors to swap cloth for fish, fish for pots, or pots for potatoes.

Buyers and sellers crowd a traditional open-air market in Chinchero, Peru.

plishments, in addition to building himself a house, included increasing the size and style of the Intihuasi and building the Acllahuasi (a kind of convent), creating public markets, building roads, and beginning to establish the Inca administrative system.

The Acllahuasi became the home of the *acllas*, holy or chosen women. It became known as a center of fine weaving, and the cloth produced here was used in religious rites, to dress priests and nuns, and for the Inca chief's family. The women also made beer and served as priestesses for religious rites. Since the chosen women were well trained and among the most beautiful women of the empire, many became secondary wives for Inca nobles.

As the population grew, Cuzco expanded and much of the population moved farther from the center of town. Lloque Yupanqui realized that a better means of travel was essential and ordered roads built between the suburbs and center of Cuzco. With better travel, the Inca chief and his administrators could continue to keep closer watch on citizens living at the edge of the empire.

Lloque Yupanqui initiated the Inca civil service system to help him oversee the welfare of his subjects. He appointed *curacas* (men who were professional government employees) to assign work, collect taxes, and oversee civil projects such as building roads and irrigation systems. The *curacas* became the foundation of the extensive Inca oversight program, with skills and knowledge passed from father to son, since the occupation of *curaca*, like all occupations under the Incas, was hereditary.

Once the roads were built and the *curacas* in place, Lloque Yupanqui went on an inspection tour. He believed that a good ruler personally observed how his citizens lived and his administrators worked. Future Inca chiefs followed his example, taking a hands-on approach to governing.

Lloque Yupanqui instilled spirit and vision in his successor, Mayta Capac (r. c. 1288–1318). The new ruler established a school system among Inca nobility, encouraged religious tolerance, and conquered the people of Tiahuanaco. Early in his reign, Mayta Capac decided that princes needed to learn about government and warfare. The schools he founded offered a limited curriculum that ensured future rulers would be prepared for leadership and government administrators would understand the general workings of the Inca civil service. The school concept expanded to include sons of the Inca chief's relatives, *curacas*, and rulers whose tribes or clans had been absorbed into the Inca Empire.

At a time when some European rulers forced their subjects to follow the tenets of the dominant religion or suffer dire consequences, Mayta Capac realized that different cultures honored their gods with the same reverence as the Incas felt toward their own gods. He wanted conquered people to worship the Inca gods, but he also allowed them to pursue their personal beliefs.

Mayta Capac recognized the importance of skilled warriors, since the Inca Empire spent a fair amount of time protecting itself from invasion and expanding its holdings by conquering others. During his reign, about one-fifth of the population served in the military, although this was not a large number of men. The empire's population stood at about 1,000 people, so Mayta Capac's army numbered about 200. To increase the efficiency of the military in moving from place to place, Mayta Capac improved roads to all outlying regions.

Mayta Capac's greatest contribution to the Inca Empire was the assimilation of the Tiahuanacos, a culture of superb builders and masons. The Incas learned and adapted Tiahuanaco skills with stone cutting, shaping, and building, and applied that knowledge to erecting stronger stone structures.

Some people were born to greatness, and others achieve greatness by their good looks. Such was the case with Capac Yupanqui, who was not first in line to succeed his father, Mayta Capac. Unfortunately for the designated heir apparent, he was too ugly to be Inca chief. The Inca chief was believed to be the son of the sun, and how could a truly homely person represent the sun god? The people decided that Capac Yupanqui made a better-looking king, and the designated heir fell into oblivion.

Capac Yupanqui looked westward toward the Pacific Ocean for expansion. There were many cultures along the coast, including powerful warrior states and clans of artisans and craftspeople. Capac Yupanqui prepared his army to move from the higher, colder, wetter Andes to fight in the lower, hotter, dryer altitude of the coastal cultures. Then, culture by culture, he proceeded on his plan of expansion by conquest. Some cultures were happy to join the Inca Empire, while others fought against the Inca army—and lost. Within a few weeks, Capac Yupanqui had engulfed the coastal region and brought nearly 120,000 square miles of territory under his rule.

Under Capac Yupanqui, the Intihuasi and Acllahuasi became temples of solid stone. Cuzco expanded, as it had since the days of Manco Capac, with groves of trees and gardens, public plazas, and recreational areas. His wife, Coya Cusi Hilpay, took an interest in the environment and promoted replanting forests and gardens throughout the empire. Equally important, Capac Yupanqui recognized the growing need for fresh water. He promoted a variety of water-related projects, including bridges, aqueducts, canals, drains, and sewer lines.

While the empire flourished under Capac Yupanqui, his household was filled with intrigue and scheming driven by ambition. Capac Yupanqui had many wives, including Cusi Hilpay and Cusi Chimbo. Normally, the future sapa inca would be chosen from the sons of the *coya*, the primary wife.

Mistaken Credit

When the Spanish arrived in Peru, they marveled at the skill of Inca builders. According to Father Bernabé Cobo, "What amazes us the most when we look at these buildings is to wonder with what tools and apparatus could they take these stones out of the rocks in the quarries, work them, and put them where they are without implements made of iron, nor machines with wheels, nor using either the ruler, the square, or the plumb bob, nor any of the other kinds of equipment and implements that our artisans use."

To give credit where it is due, the Incas learned these skills from the Tiahuanacos. It was the Tiahuanacos who developed the skill of putting two stones together so tightly that a person could not slide a knife between the rocks. The Incas simply had the good sense to borrow quality technology and the audacity to claim that technology as their own.

However, jealousy among the wives did occur. An ambitious secondary wife could hope to achieve the throne for her favorite son. This is what happened in Capac Yupanqui's court. Hilpay's father was *curaca* of Anta, a powerful and influential region. Chimbo was jealous of Hilpay and arranged for Hilpay's son Quispe Yupanqui, who was direct heir to the throne, to be murdered. Capac Yupanqui disappeared at about the same time, and most historians believe he, too, was assassinated. Chimbo's supporters named her son Inca Roca, another of Capac Yupanqui's sons, to be the new ruler.

Inca Roca did not want to suffer the same fate as his father and brother. Immediately after taking power, he married Cusi Chimbo, his mother and conspirator in the assassinations of his father and half brother, this ensuring that her children would succeed to the throne. Inca Roca became the most productive of the early Inca chiefs and the first ruler to use the title inca. He chose to be called the sapa inca, which means "unique chief."

Inca Roca was interested in road building, city planning, architecture, and improving water works in the Inca Empire. One of his first efforts was the total reorganization of the Inca political and social structure. He divided the government administration into two sections: upper and lower segments, with all political, military, and social matters falling under his direct authority. He named many people from his own family line to government and social positions. Only the priests of the Intihuasi remained directly descended from Manco Capac.

Inca Roca finished draining the marshes, a project begun by Sinchi Roca. He ordered canals built to provide ample fresh water to two city districts. In addition, he built a reservoir to store fresh water for home and crop use, which increased the number of fields that could be farmed.

Roads continued to be a major Inca undertaking. The Incas had only two means of transportation: by foot or by litter (a small carriage carried by several men). Since only Inca nobles and *curacas* were allowed to ride by litter, almost everyone walked. Llamas were used as pack animals but were too small to carry humans, since they can only carry about 100 pounds.

Inca Roca's successor, Yahuar Huacac had none of his father's ambition, vision, or productivity. Instead, he preferred to remain in his palace and enjoy a mercifully dull and uneventful reign. According to legend, Yahuar Huacac was kidnapped when he was eight years old, and this event psychologically damaged him for life. He was so ineffective that he did not even arrange the building of his own palace.

One Spanish historian, Garcilaso de la Vega, claimed that Yahuar Huacac managed to raise an army of nearly 20,000 men, but de la Vega's claim is an exaggeration. The population of Cuzco at the time was roughly 4,200 people, including many women, children, and men too old to fight. Yahuar Huacac could count possibly 1,000 men eligible for military service. Even adding recruits from neighboring towns and conquered people, the largest army possible would be about 2,500 soldiers. It mattered little, since Yahuar Huacac's army did not fight, conquer, or advance.

Perhaps it was Yahuar Huacac's timidity and lack of leadership that made his heir, Huiracocha, go down in history as the eighth and most cowardly sapa inca. His failure to face an invading army of Chanca warriors negated any efforts and accomplishments of his reign.

Huiracocha's approach to expanding the empire was one of conquer and absorb—as long as the expansion was neither exhaustive nor overly dangerous. In many past situations, the victorious Inca army looted the conquered villages, killed civilians, and acted recklessly. Huiracocha did not want to lose the wealth and value held in conquered towns. He scooped up smaller cultures and incorporated them under his authority, retaining their wealth and using their labor force.

One legend claims that after a long military campaign, Huiracocha and his son Urco Inca, his designated heir, took a vacation in the mountains. The Chanca people chose this time to attack the Inca Empire. Huiracocha felt that he could no longer rule and gave up his throne to Urco Inca, who was not up to the task of defeating the marauding Chancas. Another tale is less generous, claiming that facing the onslaught of the Chanca, father and son both fled out of cowardice.

They left the protection of Cuzco to a younger son of Huiracocha, Cusi Yupanqui. Cusi Yupanqui not only defeated the Chanca, but he went on to become the greatest of the Inca rulers, a true sapa inca.

CHAPTER 2

The Empire at Its Greatest

LEGEND AND MYSTERY SHROUDS THE HISTORY OF EVEN the greatest of the Inca rulers. The story of how Cusi Yupanqui became the military leader of the Inca army, defeated the Chanca, and claimed the title sapa inca actually began with a vision. According to the writings of Father Bernabé Cobo, the sun god Inti spoke to young Cusi Yupanqui, saying, "Come here, my child, have no fear, for I am your father the sun. I know that you will subjugate many nations and take great care to honor me and remember me in your sacrifices." The sun god presented images of the lands and people Cusi Yupanqui would conquer. Cusi Yupanqui lived in a time and culture where such visions were taken seriously, and events unfolded that granted him an opportunity to turn his vision into reality.

According to the *cronistas*, the legend began as follows: In 1438, Cuzco came under attack from the warlike Chancas, a violent, belligerent culture much feared by the Incas. To escape capture and possible torture, the sapa inca Huiracocha and his heir apparent, Urco Inca, fled to a stronghold in the Andes. This left younger son Cusi Yupanqui to defend the empire.

At this point, fact and fiction mingle. As the Chancas prepared their attack, Cusi Yupanqui dressed in the skins of a puma (an animal the Inca culture revered for its strength and cunning). Cusi Yupanqui led his soldiers against the Chanca and, as the legend goes, the sun god Inti caused the stones on the battlefield to rise as warriors and assist Cusi Yupanqui in defeating the dreaded Chancas.

The young warrior saved Cuzco from defeat, then forced his father to abdicate. After casting aside his cowardly brother, Cusi Yupanqui declared himself sapa inca. From that time on he was called Pachacuti—the earthshaker.

OPPOSITE
Inca Walls, Modern Street
Pedestrians walk down Calle Hatunrumiyoc, a street in modern Cuzco. The street is bordered by stone walls from an Inca palace.

Inca Military Might

With his throne secure, Pachacuti embarked on a military campaign to expand the empire. He had inherited a well-disciplined and experienced army. Every adult male between ages 25 to 50 had military training, and part of the manhood rituals included getting weapons of war as gifts and learning to use them. A well-equipped warrior wore padded cloth armor and a helmet, and carried a spear, mace, sling, and shield.

The military was organized in a similar way to a modern army. The Incas based their structure on decimal units; thus, a troop of 10 men had a troop leader, like today's corporal. Five groups of 10 had an officer similar to a sergeant, and units increased accordingly, with officers over groups of 100, 500, 1,000, 5,000, and 10,000 warriors. The sapa inca served as commander-in-chief of the army, just as the president of the United States is in charge of the military today. Although most officers were appointed nobles, the military was one area in which commoners could rise through the ranks. An outstanding warrior was rewarded regardless of his position in the public sector.

The Incas recognized the value of a continuous supply chain for military operations. Roads stretched to the limits of the Inca realm, and along the roads were storehouses from which the soldiers were fed, clothed, and rearmed. In addition, llamas followed the army in pack trains, carrying additional supplies the warriors might need.

Military strategy was simple: The Inca forces were divided into three groups. The first group attacked from the front while the other two groups circled to attack the rear flanks. If the enemy retreated to a fortress, the Incas lay siege to the site, cutting off water, food supplies, and communications.

According to Albert Marrin in his book *Inca and Spaniard: Pizarro and the Conquest of Peru*, "The Inca approached the enemy in mass formations thousands strong. As they came within earshot, they set up an ear-splitting racket; noise boosted their own courage and made the enemy jittery. Warriors blew conch-shell trumpets and bone whistles. They shook gourd rattles and beat drums covered with human skin. Men danced wildly, whirling, jumping, shouting. They boasted of their courage and jeered at the enemy as cowards. Some units bellowed a bloodcurdling rhyme:

> *We'll drink chicha from your skull*
> *From your teeth we'll make a necklace*

From your bones, flutes
From your skin we'll make a drum
And then we'll dance.

Many enemies gave up before the fighting had even begun.

In battle, the Inca army lined up according to weaponry. The first row of skilled sling throwers could fell opponents by hurling their smooth stones. Then followed common warriors with clubs, spears, and stone or metal clubs, and nobles armed with sharp battleaxes made of copper.

As new cultures were conquered, the Incas added the weapons of those cultures to their arsenal. Bolas (ropes with three stones attached) were one such addition. When the bolas were spun around, then hurled, the stones encircled the arms or legs of an enemy, literally tying him up. Another welcome addition was the bow and arrow. The Incas had no archery skills, but their subjects from the Amazon region achieved such great accuracy with bows and arrows that they could shoot birds in flight.

CONNECTIONS >>>>>>>>>>>>>>>>>>

Mobile Army Medicine

In modern warfare, medical teams accompany almost every fighting force. They set up field hospitals to handle the wounded. Hundreds of years ago, Inca doctors did exactly the same thing. Much like the military medicine of today, pain relief and stopping blood loss were primary concerns of Inca army medicine.

Some of the same medicines are still used in emergency medical care. Inca doctors used cocaine as a pain reliever. Contemporary medicine uses cocaine derivatives (Novocain and Xylocain) for the same purpose. Quinine continues to be an excellent fever reducer. Chilca, a natural plant substance, reduces swollen tissue around joints.

The Incas knew that skilled medical care, delivered quickly could save lives. Present-day emergency medical care and military field medicine operate the same way: stop the pain; stop the bleeding; save the patient.

As sapa inca and commander-in-chief of the military, Pachacuti declared that destruction in conquest was unacceptable. He forbade his soldiers from razing towns, massacring the enemy, or burning crops. Instead, as he annexed land, Pachacuti augmented the Inca labor force with farmers, soldiers, artisans, and experienced leaders. Defeated cultures that declared allegiance to Pachacuti were immediately integrated into the Inca civil system. Those who remained hostile met a brutal fate: Their skulls became drinking vessels, their skins were stretched over military drums, and their bones were honed into flutes.

The sapa inca approached every conquest extending a hand of friendship and offering a caravan laden with gifts. His open diplomacy encouraged acceptance of Inca rule while reducing the costs in lives and supplies consumed by major battles. Pachacuti offered gifts of gold and cloth, and guaranteed peace to those who swore their allegiance to the Inca Empire. Not surprisingly, less powerful cultures chose assimilation over annihilation.

In 1463, Pachacuti decided to forgo the rigors of constant military action and turn his hand to administering his now vast empire. He named his son Tupac Yupanqui as the new commander-in-chief of the military. Over four decades, father, son, and grandson Huayna Capac increased the Inca Empire to stretch roughly 3,400 miles north to south along the Andes. The Incas controlled all the land from the Pacific Ocean to the eastern piedmont of the Andes and the Amazon rainforest.

Pachacuti epitomized the benevolent dictator. He understood the need for defeated people to keep their dignity and heritage intact, lest they become rebellious. He appreciated certain basic needs of people—food, clothing, and shelter—and the civil administration of Pachacuti's reign bore the responsibility of securing fundamental necessities for all citizens.

However, Pachacuti was no mere idealist. As the empire expanded, he needed to maintain control over a greater number of conquered people. One way to keep potential rebellion in check was by bringing a conquered culture's principal idols to the Coricancha, the central temple in Cuzco, which had replaced the Intihuasi (see the box on page 31).

Ostensibly, Pachacuti honored these gods, and, in fact, the Incas occasionally accepted new gods into their own beliefs. However, moving idols to Cuzco symbolically held a defeated culture's beliefs captive. In war, armies brought idols of their primary gods into battle as a safeguard against the enemy. These idols were not merely images, but were believed to be fully invested with the power of the god they represented. Thus, an army automatically lost the battle when its idol was captured. Once Pachacuti held a culture's idols in Cuzco, its people would not dare rebel, lest Pachacuti order their principal icons destroyed.

In the same way, Pachacuti ensured loyalty among the leaders of a vanquished culture by providing the leaders' sons with an education. The former leaders continued to govern their people while their sons went to Cuzco to study and learn Inca customs. As an act of benevolence, education ensured an excellent (and Inca) future for the heirs. However, the sons were also hostages of Pachacuti, who would not have hesitated to execute them if their fathers rebelled.

The Land of the Four Quarters

As the empire expanded, the land incorporated under the sapa inca's rule came to be called the Land of the Four Quarters, Tahuantinsuyu. The quarters—Chichaysuyu (north), Antisuyu (east), Collasuyu (south), and Cuntisuyu (west)—were distinctly different in region, climate, earlier civilizations, and agriculture. At the heart of the empire stood Cuzco, the government's capital and religious focal point. In ancient Europe, all roads led to Rome. In the land of the Incas, all roads led to Cuzco (see page 32).

On a modern map of South America, Tahuantinsuyu would include Ecuador and the southern section of Colombia, portions of Bolivia, Argentina, and Chile, and most of Peru. Each quarter had its own capital, mode of dress, crops, languages, art forms, and religious beliefs. Yet all followed the laws and cultural patterns of Inca life. Each region had a hierarchy of government administrators to assign work, enforce the peace, collect taxes, and oversee the welfare of the people under their jurisdiction.

Each segment was under the guidance of an *apu*, or regional head. Below the *apus* were several layers of *curacas*, or district prefects. The Inca Empire based its rule on decimal units, so every group of 10 households had a leader. Groups of 50 households reported to a more important foreman, and so on up the line. Prefects (chief officers)

A New Golden Temple

The Coricancha had replaced the Intihuasi as the Incas' principal house of worship. The adobe Intihuasi was replaced by a stronger stone structure, the foundations of which are still in existence. The name *Coricancha* means the "place of gold," which was an understatement for this temple. The walls and ceilings were literally lined with golden plaques, plates, and statues. The representation of the principal deity, the sun god Inti, was a human face surrounded by many rays of light, all presented in shining gold.

31

The Inca Empire

The empire changed its borders somewhat under various sapa incas, but always had its heart in the Andes Mountains.

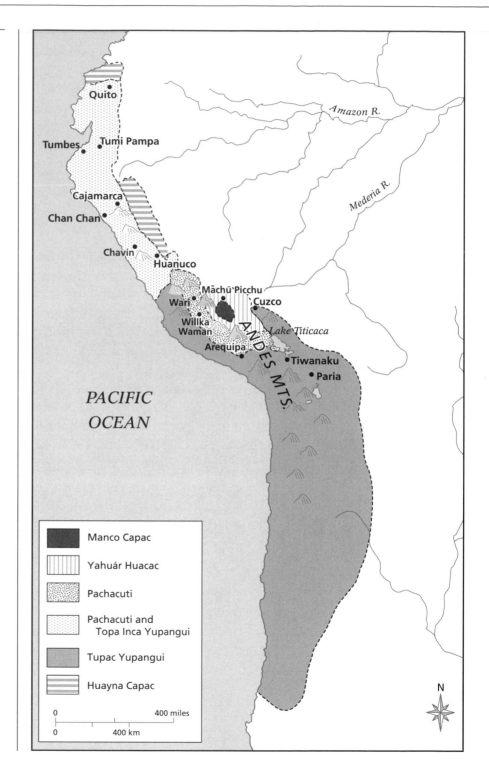

Legend:
- Manco Capac
- Yahuár Huacac
- Pachacuti
- Pachacuti and Topa Inca Yupangui
- Tupac Yupangui
- Huayna Capac

0 — 400 miles
0 — 400 km

watched over increasingly larger groups: 100, 500, 1,000, 5,000, and 10,000 households.

As the empire grew, Pachacuti realized that he did not have enough capac incas (nobles who were directly descended from Manco Capac) to administer his government. To fill in the gaps, Pachacuti instituted a new level of nobles—hahua incas, who were nobles appointed to their rank by the sapa inca. Men who had served the sapa inca well, leaders from conquered cultures, and military officers could be appointed to the aristocratic rank of hahua inca.

Occasionally, pockets of resistance needed to be quelled. Pachacuti used a concept called *mitima* to eliminate dissension. *Mitima* means "resettlement." An entire village or sections of that village were forcibly moved from their home to new, pro-Inca locations. *Mitima* broke up the rebels yet did not deprive the village of needed services, since loyal Inca workers moved in to replace the rebels and maintain normal levels of productivity.

Mitima was also used for some agricultural groups. There are several cases where villages designated for resettlement were moved to places that the Inca wanted to rework and develop, such as the terraced maize fields in Cochabamba.

Climate and Agriculture

The Inca Empire began and expanded high in the Andes Mountains. The mountains form three distinct ranges: the Cordillera Oriental to the east, the Cordillera Occidental to the west, and the Cordillera Central. Broad, sweeping valleys carved by the region's major rivers spread between the different mountain ranges. The region is broken up into four distinct climate zones: the *yunga*, the *quechua*, the *suni*, and the *puna*. Each zone supports different plants and animals, although some species can survive in several zones. Just as in Inca times, today's Andean people cope with extreme climate changes and high altitudes.

The *yunga* zone rises from the foothills of the Andes up to 5,000 feet. The region incorporates the western foothills and is generally warmer and drier than other Andes regions. In this region, the Incas built raised fields crisscrossed with irrigation ditches for increased crop yields. In its natural state, the *yunga* is a semi-arid grassland with low shrubs, cactus, and tussock grasses. However, civilizations that lived long before the Incas cleared the land for agriculture. Corn, potatoes, beans, fruit, and grain—the predominant crops of the Inca culture—continue to provide subsistence living for today's Peruvian farmers.

The *quechua* zone begins where the *yunga* ends, rising from about 5,000 to 11,500 feet. Early cultures transformed forest into farmland in the *quechua* zone. The region has moderate temperatures with adequate rainfall, and common crops in the *quechua* are the same today as they were in the Inca days: many varieties of corn and potatoes, quinoa, amaranth (a type of grain), squash, lima beans, and fruit.

Above the *quechua* zone lies the *suni*, soaring more than 11,500 feet above sea level. Mountain valleys lie above the treeline but they are not barren; they once supported vast grasslands that were cleared for planting high-altitude crops. Common crops in the *suni* include corn, potatoes, oca (a root vegetable), grains, and other hardy crops. As in Inca days, natives in the *suni* today herd llamas and alpacas. Temperatures are far colder in the *suni* than in the lower zones. Soaring above the *suni* is the *puna*, a cold zone where few crops grow.

In the east the Andes drop into dense Amazon rainforest, where the land has changed little

Farming the Steep Slopes
The ruins of terraced farms and storehouses line the hillsides of Machu Picchu. Much of the terraced farmland built by the Incas is still used today.

since the days of Inca rule. Inca farmers knew how to grow high-altitude crops in regions with limited rainfall. The dense tropical atmosphere of the Amazon must have seemed like a steambath where rain fell inches at a time and rivers flooded their banks.

The Incas used some of this land to grow coca, a medicinal herb used to improve stamina and reduce pain. The oppressive jungle was so abhorrent to the Inca people that being sent to the coca fields was considered a bitter punishment. However, the region produced a variety of unusual fruits and vegetables prized by the Incas: manioc (a root vegetable), sweet potatoes, avocados, guavas, and pineapples. These foods continue to be staples for many of the groups of Native peoples who live in the Amazon region.

Toward the southern end of the empire, the mountains fall away into sweeping grasslands, called pampas, much like the tallgrass prairies of North America. The grasses in this region send roots several feet into the soil. Inca farmers had only primitive wooden ploughs, operated by forcing the blade into the soil with the foot. With just these foot ploughs, Inca farmers had great difficulty cutting through the thick native grasses to clear land for crops. Thus, the most densely packed grasslands were left intact and thrive today as one of the world's most valued natural grassland ecosystems.

The western quarter lay along South America's western coast. It is an odd place where the world's driest desert (the Atacama) nestles up against the world's largest ocean (the Pacific). The region lies below the Equator, so winds blow from east to west. Rain clouds travel from the Brazilian and Argentinean coasts toward the Andes Mountains to the west, dumping rainfall on the dense tropical forests. Farther west, the mountains block

CONNECTIONS >>>>>>>>>>>>>>>>>>>>>>>>>>>>>>>>>

Applying Inca Agricultural Technology

The Incas used every possible square foot of arable land to produce food, and developed techniques of transforming unusable land through terracing, raised platforms, dredging, and irrigation. Literally millions of hours of labor were spent clearing land, erecting stone walls, and filling the terraces with topsoil. Present-day agronomists wondered if all that work produced good results.

In 1983, Dr. Clark Erickson of the University of Pennsylvania headed up a team of agronomists and archaeologists in an experiment to duplicate Inca agricultural methods. They replicated Inca terrace beds and grew crops traditional to Inca farming: potatoes and quinoa. The results astounded the scientists. Normal potato crops for similar acreage would yield about eight tons of potatoes per acre. The 1984 potato crop in the Inca beds produced more than 16 tons per acre, and the following year produced 30 tons per acre.

Little wonder that many Inca-built agricultural terraces are still in use today. Space-saving and effective, Andes farmers continue to get high crop yields from an agricultural plan devised in the 1400s.

rainfall from the western desert regions, leaving a desert so dry that even cactus cannot survive and corpses dehydrate into natural mummies.

Small rivers such as the Tambo, Ica, and Santa, cut fertile valleys through the dry western region. The rivers served as the lifeblood for cultures settling in the region, where by 3,000 B.C.E. people had cleared forest to expand cropland. Extensive farming began long before the Incas ruled the region.

Communications

When an empire expands to the size of the Inca Empire, there can be problems with communications. To overcome this problem, Pachacuti ordered that all people under his rule must know how to speak Quechua. They could continue speaking their own language in their everyday lives, as long as they knew the language of the Incas. Children began learning Quechua at birth. Within a short time, all Inca citizens could speak with one another, regardless of background or rank.

Roughly 15,000 miles of roadways connected the various districts of the empire. To keep communications open between each region, the Inca culture established an on-foot version of the Pony Express. Runners, called *chasquis*, were stationed at short intervals along the roads. The *chasquis* were trained to memorize and deliver verbal messages exactly as they were given. The runners traveled by day and night, so a message could be sent from the farthest reaches of the empire–more than 2,000 miles–and arrive in Cuzco within about a week. This is about the same amount of time it takes a letter to travel 3,000 miles by our modern postal service.

Rebuilding Cuzco

Once Pachacuti had delegated military leadership to his son Tupac Yupanqui, he dedicated his time to rebuilding Cuzco. He wanted the city to stand as a symbol of Inca power and skill, and he envisioned a city that would become a model of architecture, planning, and construction. Since the city lies about 11,680 feet above sea level, building projects made serious demands on workers. The air is thin, the climate features hard winters, and stone construction requires millions of work hours. By the time the Spaniards arrived in 1532, Cuzco's center included about 4,000 solidly built stone structures, with much of that work accomplished in just 60 years.

The city plan took the shape of a puma, an animal much admired by the Inca culture for its strength and cunning. The puma shape of Pachacuti's Cuzco can still be identified in aerial photos. At the puma's head,

CONNECTIONS >>>>>>>>>>>>>>>>>>>>>>>>>>>>>>>>>

A Living Language

The language of Pachacuti and the Inca Empire is still spoken by 8 to 10 million Andean people. This means that one-fourth of Peru's population and an appreciable number of Ecuadorians speak Quechua. The language has changed since Inca times, though. When the Spanish arrived in the 1500s, they devised a written form for Quechua; until then, Quechua existed only as a spoken language.

Today's Quechua has three vowels: *a*, *i*, and *u*, and, much like English, the vowels can have different sounds. The *i*, for example, may be spoken as a long *i* (bike), short *i* (pit), or short *e* (set). Spellings that appear with *e* or *o* in them are often derived from the Spanish influence on the language. This can be confusing, as both *qumir* and *qomer* mean "green."

There are fewer consonants in Quechua than there are in English. They include *ch, f, h,* *k, l, m, n, p, q, r, s, t, w,* and *y*. Spanish influence added *ñ* (pronounced *nya*), and *ll* (pronounced *ya*). Consonant pronunciation resembles English pronunciation, so English speakers have an easy time learning Quechua.

An interesting aspect of Quechua is that a speaker can indicate a degree of certainty about a statement simply by changing a noun. For example, a speaker can add the letter *m* as an ending to a noun to show definite knowledge, or add an *s* to show that the speaker heard something about the topic but does not personally know it to be true. Thus, the sentence *Tayta Amaru karpintirum* means "Amaru is a carpenter," indicating that the speaker personally knows Amaru's profession. *Tayta Amaru karpintirus*, on the other hand, means someone else told the speaker that "Amaru is a carpenter."

Pachacuti built the fortress-temple of Sacsahuaman. In the center, royal palaces and huge public plazas took shape. In the tail, homes for nobles and the central temple, the Coricancha, rose. The city had a complex sewer and water system, built with stone-lined trenches. Fresh water was drawn from adjacent rivers–the Huatanay and the Tullamayo–that Inca engineers had rechanneled by building canals. Engineers also tapped hot springs beneath the earth to provide hot baths for royalty.

The citadel of Sacsahuaman provided protection in several ways. It stood on a hill from which guards could see long distances. In case of an attack from any direction, guards warned Cuzco's citizens, who then moved into the fortress. The fortress had three major towers, one for the sapa inca, and the other two for the military. Sacsahuaman got fresh water from underground streams, and stored enough food and clothing so that a siege of the fortress would prove useless. Sacsahuaman also served as a temple for prayer and sacrifices.

The Coricancha replaced the Intihuasi built by earlier sapa incas. The main temple, dedicated to the sun god, Inti, was literally wallpapered with sheets of gold—the "sweat of the sun"—and the roof was thatched with a

Here Comes the Sun
Incas celebrate the sun festival, honoring Intihuasi. This is a drawing from Felipe Guaman Poma de Ayala's La nueva crónica y buen gobierno.

blend of golden straw, natural reeds, grasses, and stems. There were six buildings in all, with the other buildings designated as temples to the Incas' other main gods: the moon, stars, thunder, lightning, and the rainbow. Daily services and sacrifices were made to the gods in the main temple. Only priests and nobility could enter the Coricancha; the sanctuary was forbidden to peasants. The Acllahuasi—house of the Chosen Women—and the school for young men were also located in the city center near the Coricancha and the palaces of the sapa incas.

Guarded gateways controlled entrances to Cuzco, and no one could enter the city between sunset and sunrise. In the city center palaces dominated, and this area was reserved for the sapa inca, his family, servants, and the households of past sapa incas. However, when major religious events took place, central plazas across from the palace filled with nobles and peasants alike.

The city was a masterpiece of design, innovation, and planning. It had three primary districts: urban, suburban, and rural. A garden-forest separated the urban center from the outlying suburban towns. Neighborhoods or districts divided the urban area where ethnic groups, such as conquered people from the west or north, lived in proscribed areas. Their clothing distinguished them from people of other districts, since no one was allowed to wear the clothes or headgear of any other ethnic group. In this way, guards knew who belonged in which district and kept a close watch on citizens' movements. Laws prevented people from changing residence from their designated areas to another ethnic district.

Suburban towns, evenly spaced at about six miles apart, provided homes for farmers, miners, and other workers. Roadways connected each town to its neighboring villages and to the city center.

In *Inca and Spaniard*, historian Albert Marrin describes the

The Coricancha Revealed

Inca masons gained such skill with shaping and matching stones that, even today, many walls built in Pachacuti's time still stand. They have survived countless earthquakes, a brutal climate, and the destructive conquest of the Spaniards. In fact, in May 1950, a major earthquake shook Cuzco to its foundations. The 400-year-old Church of Santo Domingo, built by the Spanish, crumbled. Beneath the rubble lay the foundations of the Coricancha—still standing and rock-solid. Efforts to preserve and rebuild the Spanish church met with resistance as some people claimed the Coricancha had as much if not greater importance in Peruvian culture than the Roman Catholic church. The movement to recapture Inca heritage won in this case, and the Coricancha's walls remain.

city: "Cuzco was laid out in a huge checkerboard. Its streets were narrow and paved with stone. In addition, four main roads, one for each of the empire's 'quarters,' began at Joy Square, an open space of 20 acres at the city's center....The House of Learning and the palaces of sapa incas, living and dead, surrounded Joy Square on three sides. These buildings, made of stone blocks, many weighing 20 tons, were marvels of engineering."

A Luxurious Lifestyle

Pachacuti had his share of vanity and royal arrogance. He never walked anywhere; rather, he traveled in a litter decorated with gold and gems and carried by more than a dozen servants. Other servants traveled in front of the litter making sure the path was smooth, lest the inca be jarred during his travels. When he ate, his food was served on gold or silver plates, and since he did almost nothing for himself, his secondary wives or concubines fed him. They even collected his spit in their hands.

Gold poured into Cuzco every year, mined in various places in the Andes. It was used for decorating the Coricancha and for the palaces of the sapa inca. In Cuzco, skilled goldsmiths and artisans turned the gold into plates, utensils, bowls, statues, jewelry, and other objects.

Despite the vast amounts of gold, the Incas did not place the highest value on precious metals or gemstones. They valued cloth above even gold and jewels because of the amount of work involved in producing truly fine textiles. Cloth was worth so much that it was never cut; the garments worn by the people were woven intact, including head- and armholes. The finer and more intricate the fabric, the greater was its value. The government accepted fine weaving as tax payment. It used the cloth given in taxes for paying the military.

Women spun and wove every day, even using their free time, such as when

Royal Attire

Pachacuti enjoyed a luxurious lifestyle and was adorned with gold, rare feathers and gems.

they were walking from their homes to the fields, for spinning yarn. Weaving was done on a backstrap loom attached to the body. A loom has a warp (the vertical threads) and a weft (the horizontal threads). With a backstrap loom, warp threads are held taut between an anchor (a door or tree, for example, or even another person), and the weaver's body. The body anchor is called a backstrap. The weaver uses a shuttle to run the weft threads over and under the warp threads, working from the body forward. Thus, the length of the weaver's arms limited the length of fabric that was produced—the cloth was never longer than the arms of the woman who wove it.

Some men and religious women became expert weavers, employed by the government to produce cloth that could be used as gifts or when negotiating an enemy's surrender. Cloth became an integral part of the religious rituals made to the Inca's gods. Daily, yards of fine quality cloth went up in flames on the altars of Inti, the sun god.

The Inca ruler wore an ornately woven tunic of cumbi, a vicuña wool fabric worn only by nobles. On his head he wore a llautu, a braided crown with tassels and feathers. Thus attired and seated upon a stool made of gold, the sapa inca held audiences for his people.

No person dared look into the face of the sapa inca, as he was considered divine and the "son of the sun," and to look directly at him was unacceptable. Even the most elevated noble approached the Inca in a crouch with his back laden with a burden of some type. This burden could be small or large and represented the fact that the approaching person did not consider himself equal to the sapa inca.

Tupac Yupanqui

When Pachacuti died in 1471, his son Tupac Yupanqui became the next sapa inca. Tupac Yupanqui had already established himself a skilled military leader. In 1460, while his father was still sapa inca, he had conquered the Chimú people. This culture lived in the Moche Valley from 1300 to 1460, and, as with many earlier cultures, the Incas absorbed the best of what the Chimú had to offer.

The Chimú were artisans who worked gold and silver, turquoise and lapis lazuli. In a Chimú city, nearly one-third of the citizens may have been craftspeople producing intricate beaded collars, gold and gem-encrusted masks and crowns, religious icons, jeweled plates and utensils, and personal jewelry for nobles. Goldsmiths and silversmiths knew how to create alloys (blends of various metals) and how to solder. Artists created brilliant mosaics to decorate city buildings.

The Death of Pachacuti

In *History of the Incas*, 16th century historian and navigator Pedro Sarmiento De Gamboa describes the death of the greatest sapa inca. Clements Markham of the Hakluyt Society translated this section of the book in 1907:

Being in the highest prosperity and sovereignty of his life, he [Pachacuti] fell ill ...and, feeling that he was at the point of death, he sent for all his sons who were then in the city [of Cuzco]. In their presence he first divided all his jewels and contents of his wardrobe. Next, he made them plough furrows in token that they were vassals of their brother, and that they had to eat by the sweat of their hands. He also gave them arms in token that they were to fight for their brother. He then dismissed them.

He next sent for the Incas *orejones* [noblemen] of Cuzco, his relations, and for Tupac Inca his son to whom he spoke, with a few words, in this manner: "Son! you now see how many great nations I leave to you, and you know what labor they have cost me. Mind that you are the man to keep and augment them. No one must raise his two eyes against you and live, even if he be your own brother. I leave you these our relations that they may be your councilors. Care for them and they shall serve you....Have my golden image in the House of the Sun, and make my subjects, in all the provinces, offer up solemn sacrifice, after which keep the feast of *purucaya*, that I may go to rest with my father the Sun." Having finished his speech, they say that he began to sing in a low and sad voice with words of his own language. They are as follows:

I was born as a flower of the field,
As a flower I was cherished in my youth,
I came to my full age, I grew old,
Now I am withered and die.

Having uttered these words, he laid his head upon a pillow and expired. . . .

The Chimú city of Chan-Chan was the largest city in pre-modern South America. Architects designed the city around 10 quadrangles (four-sided open spaces) with each quadrangle featuring homes, workshops, storehouses, gardens, and reservoirs.

Chimú forts manned with experienced warriors defended the kingdom's roads. The culture supported a powerful military state with only one flaw: The Chimú depended on aqueducts to irrigate their land. When Tupac Yupanqui led Inca warriors against the Chimú in 1460, the Incas attacked by cutting off the water supply. The Chimú surrendered and the Incas took over. Tupac Yupanqui added Chimú artists and craftspeople to the Inca labor force.

As sapa inca, Tupac Yupanqui had many of the same leadership skills and foresight as his father. His name—which means "The Unforgettable One"—represents his ability on the battlefield and as a government leader. Tupac Yupanqui was a merciless, brutal warrior. Albert Marrin writes in *Inca and Spaniard: Pizarro and the Conquest of Peru*, "When the coastal city of Huarco resisted too long, he decided to make an example of those who defied him. He promised the Huarcans fair treatment in return for their surrender. But as they left the safety of their walls, he attacked. Thousands were killed on the spot or hung from the walls; piles of their bleached bones littered the ground for generations."

After a short reign of only 22 years, Tupac Yupanqui died in 1493. After his death, a number of potential leaders emerged, along with a period of infighting that ended when Huayna Capac, one of Tupac Yupanqui's sons, took charge and declared himself sapa inca.

In 1653, historian and Inca chronicler Father Bernabé Cobo, in his *History of the New World*, described Huayna Capac as an able and popular leader: "He was much loved by his vassals and held to be valiant and firm. He achieved many and renowned victories; he broadened the borders of his empire with many provinces that he added to it. He showed himself to be as prudent in government as he was vigorous at arms. . . ."

The Inca Empire reached its pinnacle in territorial holdings and power under the leadership of Huayna Capac. He led his army in conquering the Chachapoyas and Cayambes tribes of present-day Ecuador, despite both tribes having reputations for brutality and savage war tactics. Unlike Pachacuti, Huayna Capac thought that he could divide the empire and rule from two capitals. He planned to make Quito (in modern Ecuador) into a northern capital equal in all regards to Cuzco, and this plan essentially tolled the death knell of Inca rule in the Andes.

CHAPTER 3

The Final Years of Inca Rule

WHILE IN THE INCA EMPIRE'S NORTHERN REALM, HUAYNA Capac heard about strange people who had come to his land. They were white men with dark hair and beards. Since beards were rare among Andes natives, facial hair must have seemed bizarre to the Incas. The men were described accurately as wearing hats and vests of metal, riding upon large beasts (horses), and carrying weapons unknown to the Incas. The news frightened Huayna Capac, who believed in omens and fortunes. He recalled a time when he had seen omens in the sky, which foretold, he believed, of a great disaster that would fall upon the Incas. The priest who had read the omens warned that the empire, its religion, and its laws would die.

Huayna Capac believed that the arrival of these strangers to his land was the fulfillment of the prophecy, although he never actually met any Spaniards in person. In 1525, he did meet one of Europe's most deadly ambassadors—smallpox.

From 1518 to 1527, a smallpox epidemic swept across the Caribbean and Central America and headed south toward the Inca Empire. Up to this point, the Inca Empire had enjoyed a level of isolation, assimilating neighboring cultures and lands but never venturing far.

When the epidemic came, the Inca people were astounded. They had no experience with the disease, and so no immunity, no medicine to fight it, and no knowledge of what had caused such a catastrophe. The disease first arrived in Cuzco, brought, perhaps, by travelers through the region. Within a short time, the epidemic spread throughout the realm, leaving thousands dead.

Huayna Capac, became delirious with fever, and he named his infant son Ninan as his successor to the throne. Considering Ninan's age, it would

OPPOSITE
The Conqistador
Francisco Pizarro (shown here in an anonymous European etching) conquered the Inca Empire by taking advantage of the chaos caused by two brothers' battle for the title of sapa inca.

have been impossible for him to rule. But in any case, the heir contracted the pox and died in 1525 within days of his father. This left two of Huayna Capac's other sons, Atahuallpa and Huáscar, fighting over who would succeed him.

Civil War

The Inca Empire, once a mighty power, was now struggling through a civil war in which both Huáscar and Atahuallpa claimed the throne and were ready to fight for it.

Huáscar made the first decisive move by sending his army to confront Atahuallpa's troops. Four captains led the imperial army: Hango, Atoc, Aguapante, and Cuxi Yupanque. After the first major battle, Hango and Atoc lay dead on the battlefield, Cuxi Yupanque had been captured, and Aguapante escaped, only to be captured and imprisoned, then escape again.

The loss to his younger brother enraged Huáscar, who immediately sent a larger army of 15,000 to attack Atahuallpa, whom Huáscar declared to be *auca*—a treasonous enemy. The consequent battles swung back and forth like a pendulum; Huáscar sent successively larger armies, each of which was defeated by Atahuallpa and his men. Finally, Huáscar himself went to war with a massive army, only to suffer the same humiliation as his captains; Atahuallpa's army was far too experienced for Cuzco's forces to defeat it.

Cronista Garcilaso de la Vega described the final battle in about 1532 this way:

> Atahuallpa's generals had a clear understanding of the situation; their fortunes depended on their speed. So they immediately sought our Huáscar, in order to engage him in battle before he should have received more numerous reinforcements. . . . No peace offers preceded the fighting, and it immediately became a terrible melee that lasted all day. . . . The king was obliged to flee with what was left of his guard, reduced now to one thousand men, at the most. Atahuallpa's army soon overtook and captured him; and thus it was that Huáscar, having been made a prisoner by his brother's generals, saw the last of his faithful troops meet death before his very eyes.

As the new self-anointed king, Atahuallpa revealed his true nature. He pretended that he wished to return Huáscar to the throne and called the capac incas to Cuzco for the event. These nobles were the military leaders, governors, and administrators of the empire. Most were loyal to Huáscar, as they were his direct relations. They belonged to a closely knit

---

THE DEVASTATION OF EUROPEAN DISEASES

In the 1520s, smallpox, measles, whooping cough, and influenza raced through the Inca population. The population dropped from an estimated 15 million people in 1520 to about 5 million in 1548. In 2002, Peru's estimated population reached 27,949,639—still about 4 million less than at the height of the Inca Empire.

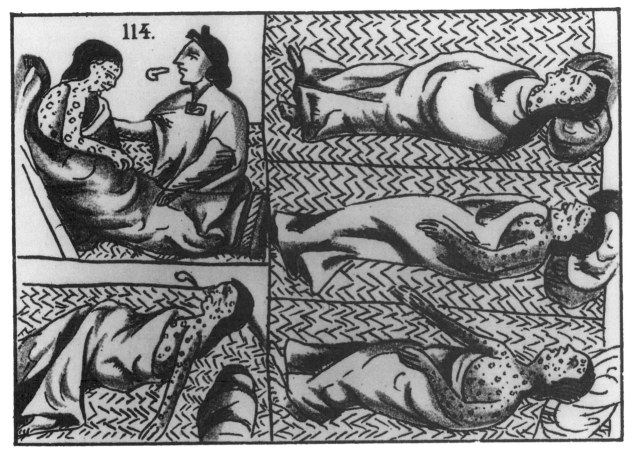

group called a *panaca*. As subjects loyal to the sapa inca, they did not re-alize they were being summoned under a pretext. All arrived in Cuzco on the set date, "except for those—and they were few—who continued to mistrust this prince," says Garcilaso de la Vega. "And when they were all gathered together, Atahuallpa gave orders that every last one of them should be put to death; for, in reality, it was in this way that he intended to make sure that the future would be his." Thus, Atahuallpa eliminated any possible claimants to the title sapa inca.

Atahuallpa also had the mummy of the *panaca's* ancestor, Tupac Yupanqui, burned. Inca subjects revered the mummies of former sapa incas as gods. After all, the sapa inca was the "son of the sun," or a living god. Thus, by destroying the mummy and principal leaders of the *panaca*, Atahuallpa destroyed any hope the *panaca* may have had of rising up again in the future.

When the Spanish arrived in 1527, they did not have to spend much time conquering the Inca Empire. The civil war had divided the

Dreaded Disease
A drawing from the early 1500s shows the progression of smallpox, a devastating disease brought to the Americas by Europeans. Native Americans had no immunity, and deadly epidemics spread quickly.

empire and created chaos. No one was certain who the sapa inca was and the political, administrative, and military systems of the Inca Empire that relied on clear directives from the sapa inca were unable to function or respond effectively to the Spanish attack.

The Conquistadors

As the Spanish conquistadors spread across the New World, everywhere they went they left destruction and death in their wake as they pillaged the wealth of Native American cultures. In 1521 the Spanish had razed the Aztec capital of Tenochtitlán, in present-day Mexico, and the Aztec gold had made the conquistador Hernando Cortés a rich man. Other conquistadors grew bitter with jealousy and greed.

Among the Spaniards seeking fame and fortune were Francisco Pizarro (c. 1475–1541), the illegitimate son of an army captain, and Diego de Almagro (1475–1538), who became Pizarro's financial partner. In 1524, the pair made their first exploration southward in search of gold and gemstones. The trek was a dismal failure. The expedition of about 80 men slogged through dense mangrove swamp, suffered from countless insect attacks, and quickly dismissed any thought that the land south of Panama offered prospects of wealth.

Despite their failure, the partners funded a second voyage, lured by the promise of finding gold. With two ships and 160 men, Pizarro and Almagro embarked in November 1526, heading toward the San Juan River of present-day Colombia. At some point, Almagro decided to return to Panama for additional supplies and men, while Pizarro and his troop camped at the river's edge.

The first encounter with Native people occurred while Almagro was gone. Pizarro's pilot, named Ruiz, spotted a large raft sailing on the river with a crew of 20 sailors and a number of passengers. The encounter sparked the Spaniards' interest because the people were dressed in fine clothes and wore elegant gold and silver jewelry. They saw drinking vessels encrusted with gems, silver mirrors, and finely woven and embroidered cottons and wool. By using hand signals, the traders explained that the gold and gems came from a land far to the south; the Spanish were dazzled.

In mid-1527, Pizarro and his men found themselves camped once more in a foul, insect-infested location–the Isla del Gallo, or Isle of the Cock. The situation grew increasingly desperate, as food was scarce, the sun burned the soldiers' skin, and many succumbed to disease. Poisonous snakes infested the swampy camp and became meals for the starving men.

Pizarro kept the men together, fishing and hunting, and gathering fruit and berries. An able, experienced soldier, Pizarro seems to have possessed an inherent cruelty and cunning equal to that of Hernando Cortés. Pizarro had tortured and burned local chiefs in an effort to get those men to reveal where they kept tribal caches of gold, silver, and gems. He apparently had no qualms about using brutality to achieve his ends.

By August 1527, the camp had suffered serious losses. A handful of men died every week, and the few remaining were more than willing to give up future wealth and return to Panama. Many prepared to mutiny against their captain, but Pizarro would not give up his quest.

The First Encounter

The first discussion between Tumbes' *curaca* and the Spanish contingent was recorded for posterity by Pizarro's secretary, Francisco de Xeres, in *The Conquest of Peru*.

He [the *curaca*] asked the captain where were they from, what land they had come from, and what were they looking for, or what was their purpose in going by seas and land without stopping? Francisco Pizarro replied that they had come from Spain, where they were native, and that in that land there was a great and powerful king called Charles, whose vassal and servants they were, and many others because he ruled wide territories. They had left their land to explore these parts, as they could see, and to place what they found under their king's authority, but primarily, and above all, to let them know that the idols they worshiped were false, and that to save their souls, they have to become Christians and believe in the God the Spanish worshiped.

Historian Carmen Bernand writes in *The Incas: People of the Sun* that Pizarro drew a line in the sand with his sword, saying, "Comrades and friends, on this side lie poverty, hunger, effort, torrential rains, and privation. On that side lies pleasure. On this side, we return to Panama and poverty. On that side, we become rich."

Thirteen chose to follow Pizarro's path to promised wealth, and they would not be disappointed. For seven months, they lived as castaways, going hungry, suffering enervating heat and debilitating malaria and dysentery. They did not know that farther to the south, the Inca Empire had greater wealth in gold, silver, and gems than any of them had seen before. And they would gain that wealth with surprising ease.

Pizarro's partner, Almagro, finally sent a ship to pick up the remaining members of the expedition. Pizarro, desperate to see the land of riches that had been described to him by local people and the traders on the raft, declared that the group would sail southward. Their arrival in the coastal village of Tumbes, near the Ecuadoran border, fascinated the townsfolk. *Cronista* Pedro de Cieza de León, who was on the ship, wrote in *Chronicle of Peru*, "When the indigenous people saw the ship coming on the sea, they were amazed, as this was something they had never seen before." The Spaniards were given a warm welcome, feted as honored guests, and treated with graciousness. The local *curaca* sent *chasquis* with a message to the sapa inca, Huáscar, telling of the arrival of strangers in the Inca land.

Capture at Cajamarca

When Pizarro first arrived in Tumbes in 1528, the empire was in the throes of a civil war. Pizarro, who had come with only a small force, decided to head northward again, leaving the brothers, Huáscar and Atahuallpa, to their dispute. In 1531, Pizarro returned to Tumbes. This time he had more soldiers, more horses, and more weapons. This larger force numbered fewer than 160 men, but Pizarro believed this was sufficient for his purposes.

While Pizarro had bided his time, Huáscar and Atahuallpa destroyed each other's armies. In 1532, Pizarro approached the city of Cajamarca in the northern part of the empire. Atahuallpa had usurped the throne and was

ATAHUALLPA, INCA XIIII.

The Last Sapa Inca
This European portrait of Atahuallpa shows him with a traditional Inca battleaxe.

camped on a nearby hill. This was Pizarro's opportunity to meet the sapa inca. He awaited Atahuallpa's arrival all day, but, as the sun set, Atahuallpa had not budged from his hilltop encampment. Some historians claim that Atahuallpa believed that the magic of the strangers—the arquebuses (guns)—would not work at night, so he waited until then for the meeting.

Atahuallpa arrived in full splendor, carried on a gold and silver litter set with jewels. A dozen or so servants went before him, sweeping the road to ensure that no pebble should jar their lord. Troops ranged around the sapa inca, filling the plaza with songs that honored their leader.

The Spaniards waited until one of Atahuallpa's captains signaled for them to advance. Pizarro did so, along with a Spanish priest, Fra Vincente de Valverde. The priest carried a Bible in one hand and a crucifix in the other as he approached the sapa inca. According to Francisco de Xeres, Pizarro's secretary, in his book *The Conquest of Peru*, the priest said, "I am a priest of God, and I teach Christians the things of God, and in like manner I come to teach you. What I teach is that which God says to us in this book."

Atahuallpa looked at the book, but the contents meant nothing to him; the sapa inca had no knowledge of any written language. Atahuallpa threw the Bible away from him, telling the priest that he knew about the Spaniards and how they had taken food and cloth from Inca warehouses and treated Inca chiefs with disdain. Atahuallpa ordered the Spanish to return all that they had taken and refused to leave the plaza until restitution had been made.

Pizarro, making a split-second decision to attack Atahuallpa, donned his armor and took up his sword and dagger. Despite Atahuallpa's contingent of more than a thousand standing by, Pizarro and four valiant soldiers advanced to Atahuallpa's litter on horseback. Horses (animals that are not native to the Americas) were strange and wondrous beasts to the Incas, and the Inca guard fell back as the Spaniards charged. The honor guard surrounding Atahuallpa was slaughtered and the sapa inca taken captive. Atahuallpa's army, with no one at the top to give orders, was paralyzed. Pizarro and his men were able to secure the city unopposed.

Thus began a bout of bravado that rivals any other in history. Pizarro told Atahuallpa not to be humiliated by losing to a troop of only five men, as he, Pizarro, had conquered greater kingdoms than the Inca Empire with the same number of men. He explained that the Christian God that he followed supported Pizarro in his quest to convert the Inca to Christianity. According to Xeres, Pizarro said, "Our Lord permitted that your pride should be brought low, and that no Indian should be able to offend a Christian."

Pizarro then demanded a ransom of enough gold to fill a storeroom in the building where Atahuallpa was being held. Atahuallpa, insulted that the ransom should be so minimal, claimed that he would give even more gold to his captives if it would purchase his freedom. After all, what was gold to the Incas? They valued cloth far more than any metal.

While Pizarro held Atahuallpa captive, Atahuallpa's men continued to hold Huáscar. Atahuallpa learned through his jailers that Huáscar promised the Spaniards even more gold, silver, and gemstones to restore him to the throne than Atahuallpa had offered, and the young sapa inca sent word to his men to execute Huáscar.

Atahuallpa's ransom weighed in at 13,420 pounds of gold and 26,000 pounds of silver, all of it in finely wrought items. Unfortunately, Pizarro saw only the precious metal and not the valuable emblems of Inca heritage. He ordered his men to melt down every plate, goblet, and decoration into ingots, which could be transported more easily than ornaments. The value of Atahuallpa's ransom, based on average prices of gold ($340 an ounce) and silver ($4.50 an ounce), would be about $75 million today. Recent art gallery offerings priced a pair of Pre-Columbian gold Inca earrings, three inches in diameter, at $17.5 million. Intact as artifacts, Pizarro's booty today would be worth billions.

According to historians, the imprisoned Huáscar realized his brother's captains had orders to execute him. Just before he died in 1532, Huáscar said, "I was lord and master of this land for only a very short time, but my traitorous brother, upon whose orders I shall soon die, despite the fact that I am his legitimate lord, will wield the power he usurped for an even shorter time than I did," (as quoted in The Incas: The Royal Commentaries of the Inca Garcilaso de la Vega). Huáscar's last words were prophetic; Atahuallpa, indeed, enjoyed only a very short reign.

With Huáscar out of the way, Atahuallpa expected to pay his ransom, regain his throne, and exterminate the Spaniards. Said Juan de Betanzos in Narrative of the Incas, "Atahuallpa gathered or caused the amassing of all the gold and silver that he had promised and as he gathered it Atahuallpa pleaded with the marquis not to allow any of his men to damage or destroy any piece of gold or silver that he placed there or caused to be gathered. Atahuallpa's intention must have been to unleash such a war when he was freed that he would once again see his gold and silver items." However, once the treasure was safely in the Pizarro's hands, the Spaniard did not release his captive.

Francisco Pizarro finally amassed enough precious metal to make him a rich man. However, after Pizarro and his men had suffered near starvation, a plague of insects, disease, and discomfort, his former partner Almagro arrived in time to collect his portion of the wealth. In 1533, the treasure was divvied up, and King Charles V's (1500–1558) share sent back to Spain with Hernando Pizarro, half-brother of Francisco.

Thus, the situation with Atahuallpa was all that remained between Francisco Pizarro and complete conquest of the Inca Empire. Atahuallpa himself had aided the Spaniards by slaughtering any other claimants to the throne and having his brother executed.

Almagro and Pizarro contrived a trial at which Atahuallpa stood accused of usurping his brother's throne, causing the death of the legitimate Inca ruler, making unjust and invalid wars against others, causing the deaths of many Inca subjects, having multiple wives, and misappropriating riches that belonged to the Inca Empire. Atahuallpa was found guilty of all charges and condemned to death by burning at the stake.

Carmen Bernand in The Incas: People of the Sun, describes the shock of the sentence and Atahuallpa's reaction: "One cannot imagine a more cruel sentence: The Incas had an absolute terror of cremation because it caused the body to disappear. So Atahuallpa agreed to convert to Catholicism on the condition that he have his head cut off instead."

Atahuallpa converted to Roman Catholicism and was renamed Juan de Atahuallpa. As he stood there with his new Christian name, Atahuallpa was strangled to death. With the last sapa inca executed, a Spanish contingent that never numbered more than 200 men took over an empire with thousands of subjects.

Spaniard Against Spaniard

By 1535, the Spanish had installed Manco Inca (1516–1544), a son of Huayna Capac, as a puppet leader of the empire, and Pizarro formed a liaison with the Inca princess Ines Yupanqui, sister of Atahuallpa. Pizarro never officially married Ines, but they did have a daughter whom they named Beatriz. (After Pizarro died, Ines married the *cronista* Juan de Betanzos.) Manco Inca remained in Cuzco, where the Inca subjects believed, incorrectly, that he held power.

King Charles V was thrilled by the amount of gold he received and he rewarded Pizarro and Almagro by dividing the Inca Empire between them. Pizarro received the northern half, and Almagro got the south, including Cuzco. Pizarro's share of the Inca booty made him a wealthy man. His newfound power made it possible for him to confiscate Inca land and riches with immunity from punishment.

Pizarro headed westward, where he built a new city at the mouth of the Rimac River. He named this city Ciudad de los Reyes (Spanish for City of the Kings), but it soon came to be called Lima. The layout of the city was quite simple: a series of relatively straight streets that formed more than 100 rectangular city blocks.

In Cuzco, Almagro planned an expedition to investigate his lands in Chile. He left in 1535 and was gone for two years. Manco Inca sent 12,000 Incas to accompany Almagro on his trip. During that time, Francisco Pizarro's half-brothers decided that the Pizarros should have the remaining riches in Cuzco. Gonzalo and Hernando Pizarro disliked Almagro, and with Alamagro and 12,000 Incas gone, Cuzco became fair game for the Pizarro brothers.

Cuzco was filled with Spanish soldiers, which enabled the Pizarro brothers to pursue their desires with no fear of the consequences. The Spanish looted the sapa inca's palace—an act which Francisco Pizarro allowed to go unpunished. Gonzalo then became enamored of Manco Inca's wife, Curo Ocllo. He demanded that Manco Inca hand her over. In a clever guise, Manco Inca presented one of his sisters to Gonzalo, claiming that she was the wife Gonzalo yearned for.

The Incas, led by Manco Inca, staged an uprising, but it was doomed to failure. They had more soldiers than the Spanish, but inferior weapons. Manco Inca escaped and headed for the rainforests to the east of Cuzco, where he ended up in the remote village of Vilcabamba. Gonzalo Pizarro pursued him for more than two months without success, then returned to Cuzco, ransacked the town and had Curo Ocllo slain. Her body was placed in a floating basket and sent down the Urumbamba River. Gonzalo was certain that Manco Inca's men would find the body, and the sapa inca's desire for revenge would then draw him from his hiding place.

In 1539, Almagro returned from his expedition to Chile to find his territory in ruins. Cuzco had been plundered by the Pizarros, many Incas had died, and a siege of Cuzco left thousands either dead or weak from starvation. Almagro and his supporters met the Pizarros in battle. Hernando Pizarro, who had long despised Almagro, ordered his enemy killed. Almagro's death left Cuzco and his other holdings open to acquisition by the Pizarros.

Continued Inca ambushes frustrated Spanish efforts to bring the Inca citizenry back under control. According to historian James Q. Jacobs in his article, "Tupac Amaru, The Life, Times and Execution of the Last Inca," "Seven of Almagro's followers…were given refuge by Manco Capac…In 1544 these seven assassinated Manco Inca, their host and protector of two years, by stabbing him in the back while playing horseshoes."

Meanwhile, Pizarro had to answer for what he and his family had done in Peru. Although King Charles V indulged Pizarro in many regards, he could not overlook the execution of Almagro. Hernando returned to Spain disgraced, where he spent 22 years in prison. In June 1541, several of Almagro's loyal men broke into Pizarro's official residence and executed him.

Spanish Dominion

By the 1540s, the Spanish were firmly entrenched in Peru. Efforts to oust the conquistadors proved futile, and by 1572, the last outpost of the Inca Empire, Vilcabamba, fell into ruin. Favoritism at the royal court gave the Spanish king's nobles land and titles in Peru. Under the system of *encomienda*, a landowner collected taxes from the people who worked the land. In return, landowners promised protection from attack. Since the Native peoples only feared attacks by the Spanish, paying tribute for protection was a farce.

The Roman Catholic Church sent missionaries in droves to convert the "heathens" to Christianity. Priests and friars destroyed Inca icons

recklessly, in a frenzied attempt to eradicate all signs of idol worship among their flock. The people soon learned to conceal their knowledge of *huacas* (holy sites, usually found in nature), temples, and religious rituals, lest the priests destroy every vestige of Inca heritage. The priests banned Inca infant, puberty, and marriage rituals, replacing Inca tradition with European customs. Multiple marriages for nobles were forbidden, along with the use of feathers, ritual fabrics, burnt offerings to the gods, and even the playing of conch shells at ceremonies. All overt traces of Inca polytheism (worshiping more than one god) were erased, as priests distributed crucifixes and rosary beads by the thousands.

To this day, reverence for all things in nature remains an integral part of the Andes culture. The people, although most are Catholic, continue to make small sacrifices to their ancient gods to ensure plentiful crops.

The Last True Inca

Despite efforts by the Spanish to wipe out the lineage of the sapa incas, sons of Manco Inca (Sayri Tupac, Tupac Amaru, and Titu Cusi) survived.

A Blending of Cultures
The Roman Catholic Church of Santa Domingo stands on the site of the Coricancha in Cuzco. It retains many Inca features, including the lower walls.

Ancient Customs in Modern Times

Today, Roman Catholicism and Inca tradition blend to create an interesting marriage custom in the Andes. The contemporary Quechua couple eventually has a Catholic marriage ceremony and is registered in the church records. Before that ceremony takes place, however, courtship and engagement are strictly in the Inca tradition.

The couple becomes engaged after speaking to both sets of parents. At that point, they enter a period of service to each other, called *sirvinakuy*. During this time, the prospective bride works for the groom's family and the groom works for the bride's family, to demonstrate to their future in-laws their willingness to meet the demands of married life. This closely follows the Inca pattern of life in which a new couple became members of the groom's *ayllu* and worked within the community. Today, the engaged couple lives together in the home of whichever set of parents has the means and space to house them. A marriage will not take place until the union has produced a child and shown that the marriage will be fruitful—and even then, weddings can be postponed for several years.

A wedding ceremony costs a great deal and parents and godparents save for years to provide an extravagant event. By the time the new couple reaches the church altar, they may already have two or three children—a fact ignored by the local Catholic priest. Once the couple is married, their children can be baptized and officially become Catholics.

Sayri Tupac established an Inca state in the city of Vilcabamba, a refuge in the rainforest.

In 1552, Sayri Tupac (1535–1561) received a full pardon for any "crimes" committed against the Spanish. The young emperor of a defunct empire accepted the opportunity to leave Vilcabamba and return to Cuzco. Sayri Tupac remained in Cuzco for nine years, where he converted to Christianity and had his marriage consecrated by the Catholic Church. In 1561, Sayri Tupac was poisoned, and the new Inca leader who replaced Tupac declared Vilcabamba to once again be a rebel state.

Titu Cusi (1530–1570) seized the throne from the rightful heir, Tupac Amaru (1544–1572). Titu Cusi became a rebel as well, attacking Christian travelers and raiding Spanish settlements. The self-proclaimed emperor had good reason to despise the Spanish: They had killed his father and brothers, and raped his aunts, sister, and cousin. He himself had been imprisoned and treated badly by his Spanish captors. As he aged, Titu Cusi became less interested in resistance and negotiated peace. He vowed allegiance to the Spanish king and became a Catholic. He died in 1570, and Tupac Amaru, the last true Inca, assumed the throne. Again, the Incas rose up against the Spanish.

On June 1, 1572, the first battle for control of the Vilcabamba valley took place. Within three weeks the Spanish had advanced into the heart of Vilcabamba, a city that lay in ruins. The people were gone, the buildings burned, and food stores destroyed. Tupac Amaru and his followers had disappeared into the jungle.

Three months later Tupac Amaru was captured and marched into Cuzco. The Spanish tried to convert him to Christianity while, at the same time, he was tried, convicted, and sentenced to hang. The Spanish tortured several of Tupac Amaru's followers to death, then hanged their corpses as a display of their power and ruthlessness.

The Inca's execution became a spectacle with thousands of Incas around the gallows, wailing over the impending death of their leader. The Spanish viceroy, seeing the crush of the crowd, declared that Tupac Amaru should be immediately beheaded. James Q. Jacobs, in his article, "Tupac Amaru, The Lie, Times and Execution of the Last Inca," says, "The Inca's last words were, *'Collanan Pachacamac ricuy auccacuna yahuarniy hichcascancuta.'* Mother Earth, witness how my enemies shed my blood.

"By one account Tupac Amaru placed his head on the block. The executioner took Tupac's hair in one hand and severed his head in a single blow. He raised his [Tupac's] head in the air for the crowd to view. At the same time all the bells of the many churches and monasteries of the city were rung. A great sorrow and tears were brought to all the native peoples present."

From 1742 to 1761, Juan Santos Atahuallpa attempted a rebellion against Spanish rule. The Neo-Inca movement arose because the Spanish treated Peruvians as enslaved people. The economic circumstances resembled sharecropping in the southern United States after the Civil War. The Peruvians farmed land that they did not own and paid heavily for the privilege. There was no way to escape the grinding cycle of poverty that subjugated the Peruvians and made the Spanish wealthy.

Following Juan Santos Atahuallpa, the Peruvian rebels threw a Spanish *corregidor* (royal administrator) and his brother-in-law off a cliff—the time-honored Inca method of punishment. The English, seeking a way to reduce Spanish influence worldwide, provided financial support for the Neo-Inca movement. However, the Spanish were too deeply entrenched in Peru and could not be ousted. The Neo-Inca effort waned, and the Spanish maintained iron-fisted control.

In 1780, José Gabriel Condorcanqui (c. 1738–1781), who claimed to be a direct descendant of Tupac Amaru, emerged as the leader of a rebel army numbering nearly 80,000. Their goals were to achieve social reforms in mining and forced labor, and to remove corrupt *corregidores*. Condorcanqui took the name Tupac Amaru II in 1771, and led his followers in repeated attacks against Spanish leaders and mine and plantation owners. Within a year, the Spanish military arrested Tupac Amaru II, held a mock trial and tortured the rebel leader.

The Spanish revenge against Tupac Amaru II was remarkable for its brutality. The Inca leader watched his wife, son, and colleagues executed. On May 18, 1781, Tupac Amaru II spoke his final words to the Spanish viceroy: "There are no accomplices here but you and I. You, the oppressor and I, the liberator. Both of us deserve death!"(as quoted on the web site "Tupac Amaru II").

The Spanish cut out his tongue then tied him to four horses to tear his body apart. This proved unsuccessful, so the Spanish cut off his head and dismembered the body. They displayed the Inca's severed limbs in the main strongholds of Inca rebellion. Their revenge incomplete, the Spanish hunted and murdered every relative of Tupac Amaru II down to his fourth cousins. There would be no more rebellions against the Spanish, no more uprisings to reinstate Inca rule.

PART II
SOCIETY AND CULTURE

Inca Society

Living Among the Incas

Inca Art, Science, and Culture

CHAPTER 4

Inca Society

THE MORE PEOPLE THE INCA EMPIRE ENCOMPASSED, THE more difficult it became to organize, control, and manage the empire's subjects. As new cultures were conquered, the Incas tried to impose their social norms and requirements on new Inca subjects. Between the late 1400s and early 1500s, the Inca army was constantly on the move. Petty rebellions became a common feature of the sprawling empire; the sapa inca attempted to control them from Cuzco. Conquered people living on the empire's outer fringes tried to oust their new rulers, but they did not succeed. The rigid systems that had brought the Inca Empire to greatness became an unwelcome way of life for some.

The Government

The government structure followed a simple plan based on decimal units. Ten households comprised an *ayllu* or clan group. Bachelors, unmarried women, widows, and widowers usually lived with a core family unit. Upon marriage, the husband became a taxpayer, a *puric*, while the wife was listed as a subject and member of the *ayllu*.

One leader, a *conka camayoc*, ensured that everyone within the *ayllu* worked and paid taxes. He also made sure accurate records were kept of births, deaths, marriages, ages of the *ayllu* members, crop yields, and wool and meat from herds of llamas.

To make sure each leader did his job, government inspectors toured the regions. The inspectors were called *tokoyricoq*, which means "see-all." They spied on everything from how clean a house was kept to the amount of work produced by an *ayllu*. Every unit level had its share of government spies to make sure no one cheated the sapa inca. This profession was

OPPOSITE
Cup for a King
The sapa inca and family ate and drank using vessels of gold and silver. This silver stepped cup dates from late 15th century.

considered honorable, since the spies prevented corruption at every level of the government power structure.

Moving up on the governmental ladder, higher prefects administered to increasingly larger units of households; 20,000 households comprised a province. "Each province had a governor who was responsible for its affairs. There were more than 80 provinces in the Inca Empire, so this added 80 or more administrators to the bureaucracy. Each governor was under the orders of the *apo* (*apu*) of the quarter in which his province lay," says anthropologist Michael Malpass in *Daily Life in the Inca Empire*.

The entire empire was divided into quarters (*suyus*), and each quarter had several provinces. *Apus*, top-ranking officials who were noble relatives of the sapa inca, administered the government of each quarter. At the top echelons of the government, hahua incas (appointed nobles) reported to capac incas (born nobles) who, in turn, reported to the sapa inca. The Inca government system was thus like a pyramid with peasants forming the foundation and the sapa inca at the apex.

The Sapa Inca

Three basic hierarchies of power—civil, military, and religious—existed in the Inca Empire, and the sapa inca was at the head of all three. He guided the civil government, commanded the military, and was thought to be the direct descendant of the primary Inca god, Inti.

Kings and emperors have always enjoyed a number of different titles, and this is also true for Inca rulers. First, there was the title *sapa inca*, which means "unique leader." He was also the commander-in-chief of the army. The people believed he was the "son of the sun," which meant he was a god in his own right. Finally, the sapa inca was also called "lover of the poor" because it was ultimately the responsibility of the sapa inca to keep the peasants safe, provide them with food and clothing, and provide for them in sickness and old age.

It was traditional for the sapa inca to take one of his full-blood sisters as his primary wife, or coya—although this was not always the case. He was also entitled to take any number of secondary wives or concubines, and some historians claim that some Inca leaders had as many as 100 secondary wives. The secondary wives were often the daughters of high-ranking leaders of conquered peoples or daughters of provincial governors or *apus*. Secondary wives were considered noble but they were not royal; their children would never lead the empire but would become part of the Inca administration.

The people proved their loyalty to the sapa inca in many ways, but the most dramatic was the sacrifice shown by the *capacochas*. In an annual event, the *capacochas*, usually children, were sacrificed. Anthropologist and historian Gary Urton, in *Inca Myths*, says, "These individuals were sent from the provinces to Cuzco where they were sanctified by the priests of the Incas. The *capacochas* were then returned to their home territories, marching in sacred procession along straight lines, where they were sacrificed. We learn from colonial documents of *capacochas* being buried alive in specially constructed shaft-tombs, and recently there have been discoveries of *capacochas* sacrificed by being clubbed and their bodies left on high mountain tops. In all such cases, the sacrifices sealed bonds of alliance between the home community and the Inca in Cuzco."

The sapa inca lived an extraordinarily luxurious life, particularly compared to the sunrise-to-sunset workdays of his people. He wore a tunic of the softest vicuña wool and adorned his arms with gold bracelets. Around his neck hung a chest plate of gold and jewels representing the sun. Gold ear plugs three inches in diameter filled his extended earlobes. Even the sandals on his feet were made of gold. Walking in gold sandals may have been a problem, but the sapa inca rarely walked; he rode in a gold-and-gem-encrusted litter.

CONNECTIONS >>>>>>>>>>>>>>>>

Lunch in the Andes

It is lunchtime high in the Andes, and farm laborers gather in a yard in front of a one-room stone house. The farmer's wife squats over a large pot, doling out rich potato soup with hot pepper sauce and *chicha*, a homemade chalky-white beer. It is harvest time, and the workers will dig potatoes and yams, and strip stalks of their corn until sunset. In the yard, women, children, and the elderly process corn cobs and potatoes for storage. This scene is not taking place in 1404 but in 2004. For those who dwell in the Andes, life today is not dramatically different from that of their ancestors. They survive by farming, eat traditional Inca foods, and battle the brutal climate just as their forefathers did centuries ago.

The sapa inca's days included daily government audiences, adding to his splendor as supreme ruler. According to Spanish chronicler Pedro de Cieza de León, "From many of the lords of the country there came emissaries every day bringing gifts; the court was filled with nobles, and his palaces with vessels of gold and silver and other great treasures. In the morning, he took his meal, and from noon until late in the day he gave audience, accompanied by his guard, to whoever wished to talk with him."

Like his subjects, the sapa inca ate only two meals a day. While he ate a wider variety of better quality foods, his main meals consisted of similar foods to those eaten by peasants: potatoes, corn, quinoa, dried llama meat, dried fish, stewed guinea pig, and herbs. The sapa inca drank *chicha*, a corn-based beer, just like his subjects. The Inca people rarely drank water or llama milk, and did not have wine.

Beyond the basic laws that Inca subjects lived by, the sapa inca could add new laws that suited his particular needs. For example, Garcilaso de la Vega says that Pachachuti "prohibited any one, except princes and their sons, from wearing gold, silver, precious stones, plumes of feathers of different colors, nor the wool of the vicuña...He also enacted many statutes against blasphemy, patricide, fratricide, homicide, treason, adultery, child-stealing, seduction, theft, arson; as well as regulations for the ceremonies of the temple."

The Coya

The coya was the sapa inca's principal wife, often his full-blooded sister, and mother of the chosen heir to the throne. The coya maintained her own household and court, complete with ladies-in-waiting. The grounds around her palace often featured a small botanical garden and a modest zoo.

While the sapa inca was the "son of the sun," the coya was in charge of the cult of the moon. Commoners often called the coya *mamanchic*, which means "our mother" in Quechua.

The coya dressed in long robes of soft vicuña wool, gathered at the shoulder with a decorative pin. Servants carried a feathered canopy over her as she walked upon a runner of fine wool. Her meals, like that of the sapa inca, were served on gold and silver plates, although the food was the same fare eaten by all Inca subjects.

Although she had no direct ability to rule and could never become sapa inca, she did have general authority over the women of the empire. She also influenced daily politics through her kinship ties in other royal lineages. Some coyas played greater roles in the Inca Empire than others. The most influential may have been the wife of Mayta Capac, Mama Cuca. Botany, landscaping, and other natural sciences fascinated her. After studying agronomy (a branch of agriculture dealing with field-crop production), she experimented and introduced new strains of vegetables for farmers. She arranged plantings around the palaces. Mama Cuca also recognized the value of fishing to provide food and promoted successful fishing techniques among commoners. To help the military, she found ways of extracting venom from snakes and using the poison to coat arrowheads and spearheads.

Secondary wives could not become the principal wife or empress of the sapa inca if the coya died. This rule kept the coya and her children safe from jealous and ambitious secondary wives–for the most part. Clearly the policy did not work in the case of Capac Yupanqui's coya, Cusi Hilpay. A secondary wife, Cusi Chimbo, arranged for both the sapa inca and the crown prince to be murdered so that Inca Roca, her own son, could be named the new ruler. Chimbo wed Inca Roca and became the coya through her second marriage.

Capac Incas and Hahua Incas

Sons and daughters of the sapa inca and his many wives were considered nobles. Although only the son of a coya could follow his father, the other sons had defined roles in society as military leaders, governors, *apus*, priests, and administrators. The various sons, including the heir apparent, went to the school in Cuzco near the royal palace. Schoolboys who had not reached maturity and passed through the Inca puberty rites were called *awkis*. After puberty, they became *incas*, which referred to their position as noble men or leaders.

The sapa inca's daughters were destined to marry other nobles, be ladies-in-waiting to the coya, or enter the Acllahuasi as a chosen woman. As unmarried women, the princesses were called *nyostas*. Once married, they were called *palyas*.

A noble-born Inca was a person who could trace his lineage back to Manco Capac, however remotely, and bore the title *capac inca*, which means "capable leader." These nobles were relatives of the sapa inca, although they could be distant cousins. Direct descendants of Manco Capac could be part of the state council, which is much like the president's cabinet in the United States. These men counseled the sapa inca on the state of the empire and ensured that orders given by the sapa inca were carried out. Four capac incas ran the four quarters of the empire as *apus*.

Hahua incas were appointed to the nobility and rose in status by showing devotion to the sapa inca or through outstanding military service. Like the capac incas, they did the brainwork of running the empire; they planned, organized, supervised, and managed large groups of citizens.

Nobles received gifts and privileges from the sapa inca, including tunics of *cumbi* (vicuña wool), which they might wear for special occasions in Cuzco. They also gained land, servants, herds of llamas, and wives or concubines selected for them by the sapa inca. Polygamy (having more than one wife) was a right only of the noble classes.

Capac and hahua incas rode in litters and used gold or silver bowls or plates. Most importantly, they were exempt from paying regular taxes to the sapa inca and the religious sector.

Curacas and Other Civil Leaders

Curacas came from the ranks of lesser nobility and from former leaders of conquered cultures. Curacas were part of the Inca bureaucracy, overseeing large groups of households, usually 100, 500, 1,000, or 5,000 in number. The primary functions of *curacas* were to make sure workers worked and taxpayers paid taxes.

Curacas had some of the same rights as nobles. They received gifts of land, servants, and cloth from the sapa inca and could ride in litters and have more than one wife. Higher level curacas enjoyed a noble's tax exemption.

Curacas had to prove their loyalty to the sapa inca and perform their jobs without bias or corruption. They were expected to spend part of their time in Cuzco, waiting on the sapa inca while sons attended school in the capital, ensuring loyalty among those curacas with sons. Daughters might be married as secondary wives to the sapa inca, capac incas, or hahua incas.

Beneath the level of *curaca* was the *camayoc*, or foreman, who served as local leader of an *ayllu*. The *camayoc* followed the work and production of people within his group. The positions of *curaca* and *camayoc* were both hereditary, and fathers trained their sons to assume their future careers.

Neither Noble nor Common

Artisans, engineers, architects, and other skilled workers fell somewhere between the nobles and the peasants. The Chimú, for example, were excellent jewelers and gold- or silversmiths and were honored for their talents.

Although these people were not required to work in the fields, they were expected to contribute two-thirds of their output to the sapa inca and the religious community.

Stonemasons, architects, and engineers worked for the sapa inca. Although they did not produce goods, their services were highly valued. Because these services benefited the community as a whole and the sapa inca in particular, architects and engineers were not required to perform other labors or pay taxes.

Commoners

Peasants lived regimented lives; they were destined to be farmers, herders, miners, or fishermen. The civil government watched over their work and provided for them if crops failed, they got sick or injured, or they reached the Inca retirement age of 50 years old. Retirement was not a matter of sleeping late and relaxing in a hammock—older people still worked. They just did not build roads, plow fields, serve in the army, or dig in the mines.

The lives of peasants were as structured as everything else in the Inca Empire; the government planned for every stage of life. If conquered people had too much free time, the Inca rulers believed, they might become restless. Since there were never more than about 1,000 Incas ruling a region as large as the Roman Empire and populated by dozens of different ethnic groups and millions of people, absolute control became an Inca imperative.

Once a child reached five years old, he or she had jobs. Girls learned to skim kernels from corncobs, dehydrate potatoes, and cook. Boys carried water, shooed pests from crops, and helped with planting and harvesting. Older girls watched over their younger siblings, fetched water and food for livestock, cooked meals, and weeded fields.

Once girls reached 16 to 20 years old, they were married. Wives maintained the house, helped with plowing and planting, processed and stored food, and produced children. Young men married at about age 25 and were immediately enrolled as taxpayers. District governors arranged marriages for people who did not choose spouses on their own; living as a single man or woman was not acceptable.

Formal education was not available to children of peasants or craftspeople. The children learned from their parents, working as apprentices in the job they would follow for a lifetime.

The two areas in which there was some upward social mobility were the military and the religious community. A young man who showed

BIG EARS

When the Spanish arrived in the Inca Empire, they called noble males *orejones,* or "big ears." It was the practice of Inca men to begin wearing earplugs when they reached puberty. The hole in the earlobe was stretched over the years to hold larger and larger earplugs, which were disks that filled the lobe holes like pierced earrings.

Woman of Gold
This gold figurine, wrapped in multicolored woven cloth fastened with a gold pin, is an Inca depiction of a chosen woman. Selection as a chosen woman offered upward social mobility for a girl.

exceptional skills as a warrior might rise to lead a troop of 10, a battalion of 50 or 100, or become commander of a regiment. In the religious community, attractive girls around 10 years old might be selected to become one of the chosen women. Those girls studied at the Acllahuasi, where they learned expert weaving skills, made *chicha* for the sapa inca and priests, and participated in religious rites. Some girls would become brides of nobles or secondary wives of the sapa inca. Others remained in the religious life, eventually becoming teachers in the Acllahuasi. To some, though, fate was not so kind: They became human sacrifices.

Mitmakonas

On occasion, a newly conquered group of people did not fit in well with the structure of the Inca Empire. The solution to this problem was to break up rebellious groups and send the people to work in a variety of locations loyal to the Inca. This left a messy gap in the workforce, which the Inca government filled with mitmakonas.

Mitmakonas were people loyal to the sapa inca, people who followed the pattern of hard work and paying taxes. It was an honor to be chosen to be a *mitmakona*, both for the individual and the community. Entire families, *ayllus*, or several *ayllus* moved into the rebellious region and brought order by example. *Mitmakonas* received special privileges, including wearing their "home colors"–the dress and headgear of their particular regions–even while living in their new location. They could also follow the ethnic and religious customs of their home regions.

The tribal or ethnic community from which *mitmakonas* came also benefited since they might be given additional land for crops or other privileges. In *Kingdom of the Sun*, historian Ruth Karen says, ". . . a loyal highland people that had furnished an appreciable number of *mitmakona* might be awarded fields in the lowlands, which its *purics* (taxpayers) could work to obtain products–fruit and vegetables that could not be grown in their own, colder climate." Of course, those new products fell under the normal taxation requirements: one-third to the community, two-thirds to the sapa inca and religious community.

Taxes

Workers paid taxes, and loopholes in the taxation system did not exist as they do today. For example, farmers paid their taxes by working the fields and pasturelands owned by the state. One-third of the crop was the *ayllu's* to keep. Another third, placed in storehouses for distribution in case of drought or famine, was the property of the sapa inca. The last third belonged to the priests and religious groups, and was used to feed the people at religious events and for sacrifices to the gods. Other occupations paid tax in a similar way, keeping only one-third of their production.

The Incas did not use currency of any kind, and all transactions used the barter system. Among the most highly valued products was cloth. Every

Louse Tax

Cronista Garcilaso de la Vega explained the Inca taxation system in *The Incas: Royal Commentaries* (translated by Alain Gheerbrant):

> In the richer provinces, shoes were made out of a vegetable raw material derived from agave plants. In the same way, weapons came from different regions, according to the various materials that entered into their making. One province furnished bows and arrows, and another lances, javelins, hatchets, and bludgeons. . . .
>
> Thus, the Inca's vassals furnished him with four types of statute labor: they tilled his land, spun and wove his wool and cotton, and manufactured shoes and weapons for his troops.
>
> We shall add to these the special tribute that, every year, the poor and disinherited paid to the governors of the territory that they lived in; which consisted of a tube filled with lice.
>
> The Incas said that this token tribute was intended to show that everyone, no matter what his station owed something to the State, in exchange for the benefits he received from it.

woman spun cotton or wool into thread and wove cloth in her free time. Cloth could also be used to pay taxes and were stored in government warehouses for clothing the poor or the military.

The government was socialist in all regards. Everyone worked, even children and elderly, to the best of their abilities. However, those unable to work were fed, housed, and clothed at the sapa inca's expense.

In addition to a share of crops or goods produced, all adult males provided terms of social service, called *mit'as*, to the government. A farmer, for example, might provide two weeks service in the army, building roads or digging in the mines. While he was gone, the other members of his *ayllu* worked his fields and made sure his family was fed. Often, if the *mit'a* duty was mining or construction, the worker could bring his wife and family. Through the mit'a, the Incas built paved roads, canals, bridges, and agricultural terraces. *Mit'a* labor supported the irrigation program, dug gold and silver from mines, and constructed government storehouses.

Keeping Accurate Accounts

Because the Incas had no written language, they developed a system of accounting or recording that even today baffles mathematicians. This system was *quipu*, which means "knots," and the government depended on the accuracy of the *quipu* at every level.

A *quipu* might be a few inches long or as much as 10 feet, with thousands of strings. Here is an example of how a *quipu* might be constructed: The *quipu*-maker counts herds and crop yields in a region for taxation purposes. There are 100 taxable households, and their products include 25 herds of llamas and a variety of farm crops. The first set of knots, perhaps in brown yarn, might show one dominant knot for the 100 households, followed by sets of smaller knots, loops, and twists to show 42 households with three children, 36 with two children, 14 with one child, and 8 with no children. The next set of knots, possibly white, might indicate 25 herds of llamas with connected knots showing the number of animals per *quipus* herd, and so on. Crops might be listed in size order: corn, potatoes, quinoa, and so on, with each crop having a specific color.

The *quipu*-maker (called *quipu camayocs*) recorded the number of taxpayers in a region, an accurate population census, the amount and variety of crops grown or products produced, and the tax paid for every bit of material grown, dug, or created. Several *quipu*-makers might be charged with recording the same territory (as a kind of backup system), and those at higher levels made *quipus* incorporating data from smaller *ayllus*.

The problem in understanding the system today is that every *quipu*-maker used different colors, knot formations, and arrangements of strings to make his *quipu*. Only the person who made the *quipu* could translate its meaning.

Chroniclers of the Inca Empire wrote about *quipus* and *quipu*-makers, so archaeologists might expect to find many *quipus* in burial sites. Considering that every quarter, province, and district had several *quipu*-makers who were constantly recording every detail of Inca life, surprisingly few *quipus* still exist. Spanish priests believed *quipus* were, if not instruments of the devil, pagan rituals that needed to be destroyed. In their ignorance, they burned thousands of records that might have provided a key to understanding the quipu.

Counting Everything
Each quipu-*maker developed his own system of colors and knots. This is Felipe Guaman Poma de Ayala's drawing from* La nueva crónica y buen gobierno.

Only about 400 *quipus* remain in existence, and they were found in burial mounds. Based on the evidence of several burials, the archaeologists were able to infer that bodies buried with *quipus* were possibly important people of the district.

The first hint of what the *quipus* meant was unraveled by L. Leland Locke of New York's American Museum of Natural History in 1910. Mathematicians continue to study *quipus*, making slow progress to understanding the accounting system of a culture that had no written language.

The Law

With social and civil structures so clearly defined, laws in the Inca Empire were few but were strictly enforced. The basic laws were:

- Do not be lazy.
- Do not lie.
- Do not steal.
- Do not commit murder.
- Do not commit adultery.

People of higher social status who committed crimes were punished much more severely than commoners were; a better lifestyle demanded better behavior. Failure to comply was not acceptable, and punishments could be dreadful. The most gruesome was, perhaps, being hung over a deep ravine by the hair. When the hair roots gave out, the victim plunged to certain death on the rocks below.

Says Michael Malpass in *Daily Life in the Inca Empire*, "Adultery among commoners was punishable by torture; but if the woman was a noble, both parties were executed. Crimes against the government were treated with special severity. Stealing from the fields of the state was punishable by death. If a *curaca* put a person to death without permission of his superior, a [heavy] stone was dropped on his back from a height of three feet. If he did it again, he was killed. Treason was punished by imprisoning the person in an underground prison in Cuzco that was filled with snakes and dangerous animals."

District officials acted as judges, trying crimes committed in their regions. Crime at any social level was rare, since the perpetrator was sure to be caught and punishment was swift and harsh. Trials usually took place within five days of the criminal being caught, and sentences were carried out immediately.

Death sentences were common for murder, adultery with a noble, and theft of property from the sapa inca or the religious warehouses. Commoners were bludgeoned to death with stone clubs or thrown over the side of a cliff. The punishment of having a heavy stone dropped from a three-foot height might bring death or serious injury.

The punishment of being jailed in the "Place of the Pit" was a death sentence reserved for nobles and government leaders. The pit was a maze filled with poisonous snakes, spiders, scorpions, and hungry pumas. The walls and floor had jagged rocks and metal shards embedded in them, so the prisoners could find no rest. Of course, water and food were not provided.

A starving person who stole food received a lesser punishment than a person who stole food he did not need to keep himself and his family alive, and the penalty for the local government administrator was even more serious. Under Inca rule, no one was expected to go hungry; thus, a starving person showed that the local administrator was not doing his job. His punishment could be loss of rank, public insult, or, in serious situations, banishment to the coca fields on the eastern slope of the Andes.

For commoners, the code of life was, *Ama sua, ama llulla, ama checklla* (Do not steal, lie, or be lazy). A lazy woman who kept a slovenly home was forced to eat her own household dirt. Her husband, also held responsible for a poorly kept home, had to eat dirt or drink the waste water left after his dirty family bathed. A lazy field worker might be tortured or whipped for failing to work, and repeated laziness meant a death sentence by clubbing.

Even marriage had its set of regulations, overseen by civil government officials. The Incas did not believe in divorce or separation; marriage lasted a lifetime. If a husband tried to cast aside his wife, he was forced to take her back. A second offense meant public punishment for the husband, and casting a wife aside three times meant death for the husband by clubbing or being thrown off a cliff. Marriage laws applied to all citizens. Even nobles, who were allowed to put aside a secondary wife, had to keep their primary wife for life.

Such punishments were rare because crime was rare. Since the standard punishment for most crimes was a painful death, few people became career criminals. Inca citizens learned from birth that their lot in life was work, work, work. They expected nothing else, so they rarely rebelled against the government's expectations.

A Life on the Reeds

At 12,580 feet above sea level, Lake Titicaca is the world's highest navigable lake and an early center of Inca interest. For centuries, the people of the region have raised potatoes on the surrounding land and fished the icy lake waters. The boats used for fishing are nearly identical in design and size to boats used in Inca times. Single passenger vessels of carefully bound reeds slip across the water, powered by sails of woven reeds or by sturdy poles in the shallows.

The totora reed has been the foundation of local life for more than 1,000 years. The local people live on a series of floating reed islands in the lake known as the Uros Islands. They use the totora reed to build houses and boats, and to bolster the base of their island homes. No part of the totora reed goes to waste, and even the roots provide a meal when roasted or boiled.

A Quecha family navigates Lake Titicaca in a reed canoe.

Trade and Transport

The Incas did not trade with their neighbors; if a culture had something the Incas wanted or needed, they conquered it. Because the empire became so large, the Incas needed nothing that they did not have. But trade within the empire was brisk. All trading was on the barter system—trading goods or services for items considered by both parties to be of equal value. The Incas had no form of currency.

Inca communities produced a variety of food for the empire: corn and potatoes, quinoa, dried llama or fish, herbs, peppers, and hundreds of other foodstuffs. Different regions may have eaten different foods, but hunger was rare. Mountain people ate more guinea pig and llama meat; coastal groups ate fish and seafood.

What trading that did occur took place within the empire at regional markets, where people traded cloth for llama skins, dried llama meat for dried fish, pottery for medicinal herbs, and so on. For example, if a woman with a sore eye needed medical care, she might pay four potatoes or a length of cloth for treatment by the local herbalist.

One factor that limited any potential trade was a lack of transportation. The Incas did not have the wheel, so carts were not a transportation option. They did not have horses or oxen to bear heavy loads; humans or llamas carried goods on their backs.

The Incas did have boats and rafts, but they were usually used for short-distance travel or for fishing. Rafts on mountain rivers and lakes were made of reeds and, occasionally logs, but they were not strong enough to bear heavy loads without sinking. Along the Pacific Ocean, larger ocean-going rafts, built from logs and sealskins, carried fishermen out to sea. They, too, did not carry heavy burdens, nor were they strong enough to travel over great distances.

CHAPTER 5

Living Among the Incas

LAZINESS WAS A CRIME IN THE INCA EMPIRE, SO WORK DOM-inated daily life. Inca subjects lived by two calendars: one diurnal (daytime) and the other nocturnal (nighttime). The diurnal calendar of 365 days—a solar calendar—set the work pattern for the empire, including specific agri-cultural activities, building projects, and warfare. The nocturnal calendar of 328 nights—a lunar calendar—determined the schedule of rituals and re-ligious celebrations. The fact that the two calendars did not have an equal number of days did not bother the Incas. What happened on the extra nights is not known.

Because the Inca Empire lay close to the equator, there were not four true seasons. Like many equatorial countries, the climate had only wet and dry seasons. However, the altitude in many Inca regions was so high that snow, ice, and blizzards were common.

December (Capac Raymi) started each new year. It was the time for planting coca, some types of potatoes, and quinoa. At night, the people cel-ebrated puberty rituals for boys reaching manhood. During this month, taxes, sacrifices, and gifts to the sapa inca arrived in Cuzco.

January (Camay Quilla) saw farmers preparing their fields; men and women worked side-by-side with wooden ploughs and hoes. The noctur-nal calendar continued puberty ceremonies, often spanning three weeks or more. Late summer—February (Hatun Pucuy) and March (Pacha Pucuy)—brought forth harvests of potatoes, jicama, and other root vegetables. At night, rites and sacrifices were made to improve corn and grain crop yields.

April (Ayrihua) found peasants shooing deer, foxes, and birds from the corn fields to stop them from eating crops needed to feed families.

Coca!

Under Inca rule, only nobles grew and possessed coca. They could and did give it to commoners at celebrations or to people unaccustomed to working at high altitudes. The coca was chewed, releasing stimulating drugs into the saliva that relieved numerous ailments.

Today, Andean people still rely on coca leaves in religious rituals and as a folk medicine. The leaves are offered as part of a gift to ancient gods and are "read" by seers who claim to tell the future. More importantly, coca serves as an herbal medicine in a region where doctors are scarce. Coca is brewed in tea to relieve headaches and dizzy spells and to heal sore throats and upset stomachs. The tea helps people suffering from altitude sickness. Herbal healers make poultices (medicated masses placed on sores or wounds) to place on rheumatic joints or bone injuries.

Coca is also the plant from which drug dealers make cocaine. Coca plants grown in Peru fall under the control of the government, and the Coca National Enterprise sells the leaves for herbal use and the manufacture of prescription drugs. Unfortunately, small farmers also grow coca for illegal sale, because one year's cocaine crop can be sold for enough money to feed, clothe, and house a large family for a year. One year's corn crop, on the other hand, does not feed the family for a full winter.

Farmers pounded loud drums and hurled pebbles at hungry birds with their slings to protect crops as they ripened for harvest. At night, commoners took part in ceremonies to honor their leader, the sapa inca. May (Aymoray Quilla) brought the corn harvest and celebrations much like our present-day Thanksgiving.

June (Inti Raymi) celebrated the Inca sun god each evening after days spent digging potatoes and tubers and planting new crops. July (Chahua Harquiz) was the heart of the Inca winter; however, work continued despite the hardship of cold and sometimes even snow. Meats were smoked or dried, potatoes were freeze-dried for storage, and men served their *mit'as* by building and repairing irrigation ditches and canals. Religious rituals were offered in honor of irrigation, since most of the crops eaten by the people of the Inca Empire depended on irrigation systems. It was only natural for the people to ask their gods to bless the systems that carried life-giving water to their fields.

A spring-like season crept in slowly as August (Yapaquiz) and September (coya Raymi) began the planting season. Farmers used foot hoes to turn the winter-hardened soil, planting corn seeds and early potato crops. Grains and other crops were planted after the corn and potato crops were secure. Nocturnal religious rites during this season ensured the help of the Inca gods in providing good crops and controlling the negative elements of nature. During coya Raymi, rites were also offered to cleanse and purify the capital city of Cuzco.

October (K'antaray) and November (Ayamarca) were dedicated to promoting good crops, as the people prayed for ample rain—but not too much. Historically, Ayamarca saw little rain, and farmers began using irrigation ditches to water the corn crops. This season honored the dead at a festival where mummies of earlier sapa incas were brought from their homes on golden litters and offered gifts of gold, cloth, and food.

From Birth to Old Age

Birth was nothing special and no cause for celebration. Mothers delivered their children on their own. While a mother was in labor, the father fasted to ensure a healthy birth. Immediately after birth, she washed her newborn in cold water from a nearby stream.

The newborn child was called *wawa*, or baby, and was not named for at least a year. A few days after birth, the infant was placed in a *quirau*, or cradle, similar to a papoose board in Native North American cultures. Babies were kept tightly strapped in the *quirau* throughout the day. When old enough to crawl or stand, the baby would be placed in a hole in the ground that was deep enough to keep the child from harm during the day. This allowed mother to work while baby fended for itself. Babies were breastfed but never held or cuddled, a method of childrearing common to all social classes. According to Garcilaso de la Vega, in *The Incas: Royal Commentaries*:

> Neither in giving them milk, nor at any other time, did they ever take them in their arms, for they said that this would make them cry, and want always to be in their mothers' arms and never in their cradles. The mother leant over her child and gave it the breast, and this was done three times a day. . . . They did not give the child milk at any other time, even if it cried, for they said that if they did it would want to be sucking all day long, and become dirty with vomitings, and that when it was a man it would grow up a great eater and a glutton.

CONNECTIONS >>>>>>>>>>>>>

Bring Back the Sun

In the 1940s, citizens of Cuzco decided to revive an ancient ritual, the festival of Inti Raymi. The ceremonies banished winter and encouraged the return of the sun and its warmth. Today, the feast is celebrated on June 24, when city and rural families parade through Cuzco's streets to the fortress ruin of Sacsahuaman. The Inca-of-the-day arrives dressed in a mix of shiny foil and cheap clothing. Dancers in beautiful hand-woven outfits twirl beneath the winter skies. The fires that once symbolized Inca rituals blaze for hours, as a llama appears in a mock sacrifice to the gods. The event serves as the opening ceremonies for a weeklong fair that draws people from throughout the Andes and beyond.

Mothers did not wean their children from breastfeeding until they were a year or more. At this point, the family and friends celebrated a ceremony called *rutuchicoy*, when a close uncle or grandfather would be first to cut a lock from the child's hair. Other guests cut locks of hair and gave the child or family gifts. At this time, the child received a temporary name that usually reflected events surrounding the birth. A boy might be named Hawk, Snake, or Flood; a girl might be called Silver, Gold, or Sunshine. Temporary names were used until a child reached puberty.

By six years old, children were expected to work. Boys and girls chased animals from crop fields, collected fruit and nuts, and helped with household chores. Girls learned to spin thread, weave cloth, and prepare food. Boys learned how to make sandals of grass, wool, or leather, how to plow, dig in the mines, cut rock—whatever their future jobs would be. Although children did not carry a full adult workload until they were much older, they learned from birth that play came second to hard work and laziness was never acceptable.

Inca boys became men at roughly 14 years of age, an event that was celebrated by the entire community at feast held during Capac Raymi (December). The feast, called *huarachicoy*, lasted several weeks and featured massive meals, dances, and tests of strength and endurance. Boys received their first loincloths, woven by their mothers, along with other clothing worn by adults. They also received their first weapons of war: a sling, a shield, and a mace. The sling represented a man's ability to serve in the military.

The *huarachicoy* included a trip by the boys to Huanacauri, a sacred mountain. Each boy brought a llama to be sacrificed to the spirit of the mountain. As they returned down the mountain, their relatives whipped their legs with sticks. The boys were expected to endure the pain without whining to show that they had reached manhood. Once past the puberty ceremony, teenage boys took on greater responsibility, although they still did not carry a full adult workload until they married.

CONNECTIONS >>>>>>>>>>>>>

The First Haircut

The *rutuchicoy*, or first haircut, remains an honored tradition among today's Andes dwellers, although the event now takes place when the child is about three to five years old. Friends and family gather around to assist in the haircut and festivities afterward that usually include quantities of *chicha*, food, and music. The child sits in the place of honor as each adult cuts a lock of hair from his or her head. Guests present the child with gifts; sums of money given at the *rutuchicoy* form the basis of a savings account for later life.

Puberty rituals for girls were a minor event compared to those for boys. The puberty ceremony for girls took place when the girl had her first menstrual period. The family and friends then celebrated for two days at an event called *quicochicoy*. A girl fasted for three days, appearing before her friends and family freshly bathed and dressed in fine clothing on the fourth day.

For both boys and girls, puberty was the time when they received permanent or adult names. These rituals were performed for every social class; however, only noble boys underwent the ceremony of ear piercing. As they matured, young men's earlobes would stretch more and more until they could wear golden earplugs measuring up to three inches across.

Ready or not, Inca men married at about age 25 and girls married between ages 16 and 20. Men and women of marriageable age could choose their own mates, have marriages arranged for them by their families, or have a government-negotiated marriage. The local *curaca* or leader had to approve any marriage, and regional governors performed the actual marriage rite. Members of the couple's *ayllu* or local clan built a one-room house for the couple, and parents provided household goods, including cooking pots, bowls, baskets, and blankets.

When the governor recorded the marriage, the husband automatically became a *puric*, or taxpayer. The sapa inca provided each *puric* with enough land to support the husband and wife, although the amount of land depended on the region and its ability to produce crops. The allotment, called the *topo*, might be one or two acres, but as a couple had children, they received additional land allotments. Each son might entitle the couple to another acre or two; each daughter, one-half acre.

Marriage for members of the nobility differed greatly from marriage among commoners. Men of the Inca or noble class practiced polygamy (taking two or more wives). Commoners only took one wife because they could not afford to keep more than one, and Inca law forbade multiple marriages for commoners.

Inheritance and succession (passing on the family's rank) was based as much on who a child's mother was as on who his father was, and was passed on to sons of a noble's primary wife. Children of secondary wives filled the growing need for regional rulers. If a primary wife died, a secondary wife could not take her place; this practice reduced jealousy and probably saved the lives of many primary wives and their sons.

People who were too old, too sick, or too disabled to work were supported by the government. Few people lived to age 50, but anyone who did retired from the normal adult workload. They were given tasks suited to their age, such as stripping corn from the cob, drying or smoking fish or meat, or educating children about household chores.

Widows were not required to marry again, and a farmer's widow kept the family *topo* or land allotment until she died. The members of her *ayllu* plowed and planted for her. If still able to work, she might assist in the planting, weeding, or harvesting. However, she was not expected to farm the land without help.

Rural Life

Celebrating life events added joy to the heavy workloads borne by Inca people, whether they lived in heavily populated urban centers or in remote rural towns. The Inca love for order and organization extended to the farthest reaches of the empire.

All-Purpose Animal
The llama provided food, clothing, milk, leather, and, as this silver statue shows, transport for the Incas.

Rural folk worked various jobs, such as farming, herding, and mining. Depending on the altitude and irrigation system, farmers grew corn, various types of potatoes, beans, squash, fruit, and dozens of other food plants and herbs. Men and women worked the fields together. The man turned the soil with a foot plow, called a *taclla*, while his wife moved along the plowed row, breaking soil clumps with a *lampa*, a wooden hoe.

Those who worked with livestock maintained herds of llamas that provided food, wool, leather, and pack animals. A llama could travel about 20 miles a day; greater distances were not possible, as llama handlers walked beside their animals.

Most mines were high in the Andes, where work was difficult because the high altitude meant reduced oxygen levels and colder temperatures. Most miners did not work a full Inca workday of sunrise to sunset. Instead, they usually worked only six to eight hours in the mines.

Men were responsible for doing their daily jobs, hunting under scrutiny of the local *camayoc*, paying taxes, and working mandatory community service. They provided labor for repairing or building roads, irrigation canals, and bridges, and could be called on to serve in the military. Men also made their family's sandals, either from woven plant fibers, wool, or leather, along with pottery, weapons, and wooden tools. Even the sapa inca knew how to make sandals—a skill required of every adult male.

Women worked the fields, cooked, raised the children, nursed the sick, and kept house. They spun fiber into yarn and wove cloth to provide clothing for the family and to pay taxes. There was no time wasted in a woman's day, and idle time, including walking to and from the fields, was spent spinning.

Rural children received no formal schooling, learning their future jobs from their parents. Since there was no opportunity to move up in society, they needed no other education.

Families lived in one-room houses with stone walls and thatched roofs. Since there was little theft—and most people owned nothing of great value—houses did not have doors or windows, just open entryways. Houses offered protection from the elements at night, when families huddled together on straw pallets to sleep. Eating, cooking, general work, childcare, and all other daily chores were done outside, regardless of the weather.

City Life

On special occasions, such as paying taxes or taking part in religious celebrations, government administrators and subjects headed to the Inca cities. Cuzco served as the Inca capital, but each region had at least one major city where government officials lived and religious ceremonies took place.

At a time when European cities had open sewers and garbage was dumped into the streets, Inca cities had clean running water and a complex sewer system. Some city engineers tapped into underground hot springs to provide nobles with hot and cold running water.

Expert weavers, potters, masons, and metalworkers congregated in cities to ply their trades. These jobs, like farming and herding, were passed from generation to generation. Children of craftsmen began studying for their trades at about six years old.

Even in the cities, few children attended schools. With no written language and a strict social structure that limited advancement, children had no need to know more than they could learn at home. Formal education was limited to sons of nobles, sons of provincial rulers and con-

Llama Jerky?

Inca wives were experts at preserving llama meat to make *charqui*. This meat product, pronounced *CHAR-kee*, is sold today in convenience stores and supermarkets throughout the United States as jerky (although here it is usually made from beef).

Traditional *charqui* (unlike modern jerky) consisted of seasoned and dehydrated meat packages that included bones. The Incas used the frosts and climate conditions of high altitudes to accomplish the dehydration.

Charqui preserved meat for storage in government and religious warehouses and fed families during the long Andean winters. Pieces of the meat were added to potatoes, other tubers, or dried corn to make wholesome stews. Traditional style llama *charqui* is sold in Peru's open-air markets and remains a staple protein for many who live in the Andes.

quered leaders, and the Chosen Women. Noble boys went to the school in Cuzco for about four years, where they learned history and military strategy, religion, and the use and development of the quipu. Teachers—*amautas*—disciplined their students by beating or whipping them, a practice acceptable to Inca parents.

City life was not much different from rural life in that people were expected to work sunrise to sunset. They used their homes for sleeping and performed all other daily tasks outside.

What the Incas Ate

Urban or rural, sapa inca, nobleman, farmer, or miner, Inca people all ate roughly the same food. True, the sapa inca ate his meals off gold or silver plates while his people ate off wooden platters, but they all ate corn, potatoes, grains, and meat.

Between 50 and 60 percent of the plants people worldwide eat today can be traced back to the region in which the Incas lived. The two most common and important were corn, or maize, and potatoes. Maize was not a staple anywhere in Peru until after 500 B.C.E. It first appears about 6,000 B.C.E. in Mexico, and from there spread in primitive form through Central America and northern South America. It seems to have arrived in Peru before 3,000 B.C.E., but did not become an important crop until much later. Even in Chavín it was only a secondary crop. However, in Inca times it was the staple throughout the empire. Potatoes were the other staple food in nearly every meal the Incas ate.

The Inca people ate a variety of plant foods, including spices and seasonings, such as hot and chili peppers, and several types of mint. They also ate algae, squash, tomatoes, pumpkins, and palmetto. Among fruits and nuts, Incas enjoyed pineapple, sour cherry, custard apples, cashew nuts, cactus fruit, plums, peanuts, elderberries, guavas, avocados, and an ancient form of banana. Potatoes and sweet potatoes were common root vegetables, along with jicama, oca, yucca, cassava, ollucu, mashua, and begonia. Beans included kidney beans, limas, and string beans, along with uncommon varieties such as cazza, pashuru, and tarwi.

Cereal grains common in Inca times included maize, quinoa, caniwa, and amaranth. Today, people still eat corn on the cob, creamed, popped, and as hominy grits or corn bread. Quinoa and amaranth are popular grains available at health food stores in bread, crackers, breakfast cereal, and flour. Amaranth has been added to the diet of NASA astronauts because of its important nutritional value.

Along with beans, meat provided needed protein for Inca people. The vast majority of meat eaten by people in the Inca empire came from llamas or alpacas. Guinea pigs were party food and were more important as a source of fat than protein. Those who lived along the ocean or major rivers enjoyed tuna, catfish, sardines, king fish, mussels, and clams.

Inca people used dietary supplements, much as people do today. They ate kaolin (a type of clay) for upset stomach or indigestion; kaolin is

Celebrating the Potato
Villagers cook freshly harvested potatoes in an underground pit during the June Potato Festival in Huancavelia, Peru. The festival is organized by the International Potato Center.

The World of Potatoes

It would seem that a potato is a potato is a potato. Not so. The most common type of potato eaten in the world today is the *solanum tuberosum*, which is directly traced to Inca agriculture. In fact, the *solanum tuberosum* was one of several hundred potatoes and tubers grown in the Inca Empire.

Today, most potatoes worldwide fall under one of about seven different potato species. In the Andes, roughly 3,000 different potato varieties are grown and sold. Lima, Peru, is home to the International Potato Center, where some 5,000 potato species have been developed.

The Incas cooked potatoes in stews, baked them in coals, and prepared them for storage. The Incas developed *chuño*, the first freeze-dried potatoes—a precursor to present-day instant mashed potatoes. The potatoes were sliced thin and placed in neat rows outside, where they froze overnight. Each morning for several days, ice crystals were removed from the potato slices until the potatoes were dry. Freeze-dried potatoes fed Inca families through long winters and famines, and were stored in warehouses for feeding the army or hungry citizens. They were also placed at "rest stops" along Inca roads to feed travelers on their trips.

a main ingredient in many over-the-counter medicines people take today for the same problems. Inca cooks added salt and pepper to their foods for flavor and because salt is a dietary necessity. They also consumed mineral lime to add calcium for strong bones.

Every household, whether rural or urban, produced a type of beer made from corn and local berries. The beer, called *chicha*, was made in large pottery vats and cooled by burying urns partially in the ground or by placing them in icy cold mountain streams. Inca people also drank water from clean mountain springs.

Clothing

Cloth was so highly valued by the Inca society that it was used as a type of currency, and many people paid taxes or bought needed goods with cloth. A number of expert weavers—usually men or chosen women—wove cloth for the sapa inca. The finest cloth was made from vicuña wool and was kept for use only by the nobles; gifts of vicuña wool from the sapa inca were prized. The chosen women also produced cloth used for religious shrines, priests, and priestesses. Clothes for commoners were made of llama wool or a blend of wool and cotton. People living near the coast, where it was hotter, wore lightweight cotton.

Regardless of rank, most men and women wore the same style of clothes. Men wore tunics that reached to the knee and loincloths for undergarments. Women wore long dresses that reached to the ankle and were held in place by belts tied around the waist. Both men and women wore sandals made of grass or leather that were worn year around, even through the snow.

Religion

While work consumed the diurnal calendar, religion dominated the nocturnal calendar. Every month had at least one major religious celebration and three or more lesser rites, so the Incas had 120 days of religious rituals throughout the year.

The Incas believed that the god Virachocha, who was neither male nor female, created the earth, sky, stars, and all living things. They believed Viracocha made the sun and moon by plucking them from an island in Lakc Titicaca, high in the Andes, while people and animals were formed from clay in Tiahuanaco on the lakeshore.

The Incas honored the sun, Inti, as an important god, portraying Inti as a face within a golden disk and surrounded by rays. Officially, the sapa inca was the "son of the sun," a divine being that directly descended from the sun god. Upon death, the people believed the sapa inca had returned to the sun. The major religious event of the year was the Inti Raymi, a multi-day festival honoring Inti, complete with food supplied by the sapa inca and local priests.

Sixteenth century priest Cristóbal de Molina described the celebration in *The Fables and Rites of the Incas* (translated by Clements R. Markham): "All the people of Cuzco came out, according to their tribes and lineage, as richly dressed as their means would allow; and having made reverences to the Creator, the Sun, and the lord Inca, they sat down on their benches [and] passed the day in eating and drinking, and enjoying themselves; and they performed the *tauqui* called *alançitua saqui* [a dance] in red shirts down to their feet. . . . They gave thanks to the Creator for having spared them to see that day, and prayed that they might pass another year without sickness. . . . "

Inca subjects revered a number of other gods and goddesses, all related to nature. Mama Quilla–the moon–was the honored sister and wife of Inti, the sun god. Shrines to Mama Quilla featured silver artifacts

The Ice Princess
The first frozen Inca mummy ever found was discovered by American archaeologist Johan Reinhard in 1995. She has been displayed around the world, and now rests in Arequipa, Peru.

because the people believed that silver came from the "tears of the moon." During a lunar eclipse, the people believed Mama Quilla had been swallowed up by a puma or a snake. To undo this tragedy, the people pounded drums, blew horns and pipes, and made a great noise. Their efforts were rewarded when the moon emerged from its eclipse. Priests and priestesses honored Pacha Mama (Mother Earth) and Mama Cocha (Mother Water) by offering sacrifices to them to ensure good harvests.

After Inti, the god with the most power was Illapa, who represented rain, thunder, and lightning. Pictures of Illapa showed a man's form in the sky holding a war club in one hand and a sling in the other. These two weapons were the principal weapons of the military, and Illapa was both the god of thunder and lightning and the god of war.

The Incas honored their gods at a principal shrine in Cuzco called the Coricancha. This building was made of dark stone, and was decorated inside with gold and silver; there were buildings set aside to worship the six main gods, including Inti, Illapa, and Mama Quilla. However, many holy places existed throughout the Inca Empire.

The Incas built and maintained spirit dwellings and holy places, called *huacas*, which could be caves, springs, oddly shaped rocks, or manmade shrines. Battlegrounds and cemeteries could also be honored as *huacas*.

The idea of a spiritual place stretched to include spiritual artifacts, such as amulets, statues, relics, and both animals and plants designated as holy. Thus, *huaca* came to mean all religious places and artifacts connected with gods and worship. Damaging or destroying a holy place or object was a criminal act.

The Incas worshiped the sun, moon, and other cataclysmic or dramatic events of nature, such as thunder and lightening. They believed in an afterlife. For them, the body was possessed by two different souls. Each soul followed a divergent path upon the person's death. One path lead to the person's origin—the nature of that origin depended on how virtuous and productive a life the person had led. The other soul remained in its body and would stay there forever once the corpse had been mummified. Bodies were treated with herbs and wrapped in a mummy bundle. To provide for this soul, a mummy was swathed in cloth that contained many necessary personal items. A goldsmith might be buried with his tools, a woman with her loom and yarn for weaving, a potter with jars from his workshop.

The sapa incas were also mummified, but they were not buried. The sapa inca was considered divine, a god among the living—and therefore could not really die. The palace in which a sapa inca lived his life became his shrine for the afterlife,. There, the mummy lived in splendor amid his former wives, servants, and household guard. who continued to wait upon his mummified body. During the Festival of the Dead in November, mummified sapa incas were carried on golden litters from their palaces to the plaza in Cuzco. They were honored with feasts, music, and dancing, and offered gifts of cloth, gold, and food.

Daily life among the Incas depended heavily on the fate of each person, as seen by diviners. These visionaries foretold future illness, bad luck, and criminal investigations, and also told people what sacrifices should be made to head off these forebodings. Occasionally, future events were foretold by reading coca leaves or by taking hallucinogenic drugs. Sacrifices to the gods were the only way to overcome ill luck. These sacrifices included food (primarily potatoes, llama, or guinea pig), cloth, or other handcrafts.

Religion was as carefully organized as every other part of Inca life. There was a head priest, the *uma uillca*, who would be roughly equivalent to a pope or archbishop in Christianity. Beneath the head priest were *hatun uillcas*, whose jobs closely resembled regional administrators. The *hatun uillcas* supervised the religious segments of the Inca Empire. At the lowest level of priests were the *yana uillcas*, who served as local priests and would compare with parish priests, synagogue rabbis, or church ministers today.

Priests had several different duties, including instructing local people about the gods and rites performed in the gods' honor. Priests also heard confessions of commoners and gave them penance for their sins, which could be a physical punishment, such as being struck with a rock on the back of the head. The most severe penance was a form of banishment that required a man or woman to live in the wilderness, forage in the woods for food, and keep away from other people. The loneliness of banishment was painful for people who depended on community life for survival.

THE WOMAN OF ANCÓN

The mummy of an Inca woman was found in Ancón in 1976. Her mummy was in excellent condition, wrapped in several layers of fine cloth. It was obvious to archaeologists Karen Stothert and Roger Ravines, studying the mummy of Ancón, that she had been an excellent weaver, much honored by her friends and family. In her wrappings, Stothert and Ravines found four burial shrouds. The corpse's head had been placed on a pillow, then wrapped. She wore rings on her hands. Within the mummy bundle lay a workbasket filled with weaving materials. There were bobbins and cones with cotton fiber, painted spindles, and materials for dyeing. She had household goods wrapped in the bundle. These included corn, dried fruit, beans, silver rings, shells, and valuable coca leaves.

Worshiping the Sun
This somewhat fanciful engraving of an Inca priest was done by French artist L.F. Labrousse in 1796 to illustrate a book about exotic lands.

Women served the Inca religion as chosen women. Regional administrators selected these women—*acllas*—for service by the age of 10. Physical beauty was the primary criterion for selection, and the girls chosen could not refuse the honor. *Acllas* studied in the Acllahuasi, and many became teachers for other chosen women; they were called *mamacunas*, or guardian mothers.

As young girls, the *acllas* were trained to follow one of three paths: priestess, wife, or sacrifice. A girl might become priestess of the sun or the moon, whose primary job was weaving fine cloth for the sapa inca, preparing food and cloth as offerings to Inca gods and goddesses, and participating in rituals. The most beautiful girls often became secondary wives for the sapa inca or other nobles, since the nobility could have more than one wife. The final group provided human sacrifices, although such offerings were rare in Inca society.

At the height of the Inca Empire, there may have been as many as 1,500 chosen women, which the Spanish called the virgins of the sun. When an *aclla* who was destined to become a priestess reached adulthood, she spoke vows that committed her to the religious life. The vows were significant; once becoming a virgin of the sun, the women rarely saw any men—not even a high priest or the sapa inca. If a chosen woman took a lover, the two were executed.

The people paid taxes to support the priests and chosen women, supplying the religious community with raw wool for spinning and weaving, food, leather, cloth, gold and silver objects for temples and shrines, and religious artifacts. Items given to the temples and shrines were used as sacrificial offerings or to maintain the religious people; stored food provided feasts at public festivals.

Among the many offerings made to the gods were daily sacrifices of animals and occasional human sacrifice. Unlike the Aztecs, the Incas did not believe that regular human sacrifice had any advantage over sacrificing animals or cloth, although they did believe that specific gods should receive very specific sacrifices. Viracocha, founder of the world, received the sacrifice of brown llamas, while white beasts were dedicated to Inti, and speckled or spotted creatures became gifts to Illapa.

Human sacrifice was made only when sacrificing animals did not seem sufficient, such as during major disasters—earthquakes, drought, famine, or eclipses. The most common victims were girls and boys about 10 years of age, although some sacrificial victims were infants.

Archaeologists believe the children were drugged or encouraged to drink large quantities of *chicha* before the ceremony. According to Bernabé Cobo, a Spanish priest, boys "were killed by strangulation with a cord, or by a blow with a club and then they were buried." Some children were buried alive and usually froze to death long before the drugs wore off. Mummified bodies of sacrifice victims show that clubbing and live burials were definitely used. Historians believe child sacrifices may have taken place twice a year.

CHAPTER 6

Inca Art, Science, and Culture

THE INCAS WERE PRACTICAL PEOPLE, AND MOST INCA ART was also practical. The culture admired production, not original design, and they saw no use for landscapes, portraits, or interpretive art. Critics claim that Inca art shows little imagination because Inca artists used the same themes repeatedly. However, few weavers today could produce cloth as intricate and tightly woven as *cumbi*. Even with modern tools, today's potters would have difficulty reproducing the fine pottery and glazes of the Moche. And few rulers enjoy gardens embellished with perfect gold replicas of corn, butterflies, and guinea pigs.

Cronista Garcilaso de la Vega described the sapa inca's garden: "There were fields of corn with silver stalks and golden ears, on which the leaves, grains, and even the corn silk were shown. In addition, there were all kinds of gold and silver animals in these gardens, such as rabbits, mice, lizards, snakes, butterflies, foxes, and wildcats; there were birds set in the trees, and others bent over the flowers, breathing in their nectar."

Weaving

Although every woman and many men could weave cloth, expert textile artisans were valued for their talents. In their hands, yellow, red, brown, and gold yarns came together in intricate geometric patterns. Only nobles wore ornate or patterned cloth, and the clothing of lesser nobles never outshone the tunics of the sapa inca.

Accomplished male weavers and the *mamacunas* of the chosen women produced woolen cloth made from the fleece of llamas, alpacas, and vicuñas. Cotton yarn, either alone or commingled with wool, was also common, particularly in coastal regions where wool clothing was too hot to wear. Weavers created woven, repetitive patterns of rectangles, squares, and diamonds, or embroidered animals, such as pumas, llamas, and birds, onto finished cloth.

Gold and Silver

The Inca culture described gold as "sweat of the sun," and it adorned the palaces of the sapa incas and the Inca nobility, and the Coricancha—the temple of the sun. Despite having only rudimentary tools, goldsmiths

A Tradition in Textiles

"In the Andes of Peru, weavings are important to every Inca family. Every village has its own weaving patterns. There are thousands of techniques, layouts, styles, and practices associated with Peruvian weaving. We draw on a tradition of over 2,000 years and we are still weaving today," says Nilda Callañaupa, director of the Center for Traditional Textiles of Cuzco, in "A Message from Nilda Callañaupa" that appears on the center's web site, www. incas.org.

Established in 1996, the Center for Traditional Textiles of Cuzco attempts to preserve and revive ancient textile skills. The center is a living museum in which carding, spinning, dyeing, and weaving are carried on in both traditional and non-traditional ways. Weaving has religious, ritualistic, and historical connections. The Inca citizenry honored Mother Earth—Pachamama—in the warp and weft of woven cloth. Spinning, dyeing, and weaving catalogs the industry of the civilization's women, from the lowest peasant wife to the noble coya.

The center brings weaving skills into modern education by partnering skilled weavers with community children. It rewards outstanding artistry by displaying the works of weavers and offering financial prizes for particularly beautiful work. The center also provides a site for weavers to work their craft, demonstrating hard-won skills for the public.

To record the historic significance of textiles in the Andes, the center interviewed more than 80 weavers. They documented traditional patterns and identified weavers who produce the same geometric and figurative patterns so honored in the days of Pachacuti and Tupac Yupanqui.

Nilda Callañaupa serves as both director and principal weaver for the Center for Traditional Textiles of Cuzco. She combs, cards, and spins raw materials (cotton, llama wool, alpaca wool, and vicuña wool) into yarn in the same fashion as her ancestors.

While the center offers works for sale, buyers should expect to pay dearly for high quality weaving. A tapestry made of vicuña wool, for example, might cost as much as $5,000. The price reflects the scarcity of vicuña, the difficulty in collecting enough of the wool to produce cloth, and the time invested by the weaver.

and silversmiths wrought remarkably fine work. Filigree earplugs, mother-of-pearl mosaics against a gold background, gem-encrusted knives and plates, and funerary masks were owned by the emperor and crown princes.

In fact, the emperor's household fairly glowed with bright golden plates, wall plaques, plates and utensils, jugs and *aryballos* (bottles). The Incas did not use much furniture, but the sapa inca did sit on a golden stool or ride in a gold and gem-encrusted litter. (He was shielded from the sun by parasols made of tropical bird feathers.)

What is most phenomenal is that Inca smiths produced jewelry and artifacts as delicate as any produced in Europe at the time—yet without the tools designed for such work. Goldsmiths pounded bright metal into thin sheets using only stones. They laid the gold on large flat rock, then hammered with smaller, rounded stones in their hands. The gold was heated, pounded, and cooled again, repeating the process until the gold sheet was paper-thin. Smiths also created alloys of gold and silver or other precious metals and annealed (strengthened) the metal by heating it in human-operated blast furnaces.

The Inca furnace was a technological marvel. Made of clay, Inca smelting furnaces reached temperatures up to about 1,830 degrees Fahrenheit. To reach such high temperatures, furnaces required steady blasts of air blown onto the coals. Not having bellows, the Incas used long copper pipes and human labor. About a dozen pipes were inserted into blast holes in the furnace base, and workers blew into the pipes, much like a bellows, and forced more air into the firepan.

Using sharp, pointed tools, goldsmiths embossed the gold with designs of the sun, pumas, birds, or feathers. Goldsmiths, like most other artists, lived in Cuzco and were supported by the civil government. They lived in houses, ate food, and wore clothing provided by the sapa inca's administrators.

So fine was Inca gold and silver work that Spanish conquistadors and historians remarked on its quality. In 1613, Spaniard Juan de Torquemada, stated that Inca smiths produced jewelry "greatly surpassing that of our Spanish jewelers because they could make birds whose heads, tongues, and wings could be made to move, and animals in whose paws they place trinkets that seemed to dance," (as quoted in *Incas: Lords of Gold and Glory* by Time Life Books).

The Incas's skill with gold did not astound the Spanish to the point that preserving art outweighed the conquistadors' greed. When the sapa

Practical and Beautiful

Inca pottery designs were mostly borrowed from other cultures. The bird shape in the piece on the left was popular in Chavín and Moché pottery.

inca Atahuallpa paid the Spanish ransom in gold plates, plaques, utensils, and jewelry, the Spanish promptly melted down thousands of hours of painstaking artistry into ingots, because ingots were easier to transport.

Archaeologists discovered many of the gold and silver artifacts that remain intact in burial mounds. They have uncovered silver statuettes of musicians playing panpipes, hammered gold goblets and beakers, and shiny pectorals (chest ornaments) cut from thin sheets of gold. Personal items, such as tweezers for removing whiskers and knives for cutting meat, lay among the bones of Incas long dead. These buried artifacts accompanied only nobles into the afterlife—commoners never owned precious metal items.

Pottery

Like weaving, pottery and ceramic skills developed many centuries before the Inca Empire rose to power. Examples of Chavín and Moché pottery have been uncovered in ruins, temples, and burial sites. These pieces include spouted vessels used for drinking beer, large urns and jars to store or cook foods, *aryballos*, and small statues. The ceramics of these cultures have intricate geometric patterns, figurative birds and animals, occasionally human forms, and human figures in action.

Although Inca pottery was decorated, the ideal piece was utilitarian, and easy to mass produce. The Incas used pre-fired colored slips of fine clay particles mixed with ground mineral pigments to decorate their pottery; a reflective surface (similar to glazing, which the Incas did not do) was achieved by polishing before firing. The motifs and shapes of Inca ceramic pieces were borrowed from earlier cultures. These somewhat plain clay jugs and earthenware crockery were never designed for palace use; only gold and silver were satisfactory for a ruler who claimed he was the son of the sun.

Fun and Games

For all the beauty created, gold jewelry, textiles, and pottery resulted from hard work, which was the guiding force of Inca life. Work, not play, took precedence in the Inca daily schedule, and there was little time for fun and games. Athletic contests were limited to sons of the nobility and were associated with male puberty rites. Foot races at full speed down an Andes precipice often provided many more wounded than winners, but they were one source of public entertainment. Young men also played war games, much like Roman gladiators, in which they demonstrated their prowess with slings, clubs, javelins, or bolas.

Hunting provided sport with a positive result: meat for the masses. It was against the law to hunt in the sapa inca's forests, and poachers were executed when caught. A government-authorized hunt provided guanacos, vicuñas, deer, and other game meats for festivals and for drying and storing. Hunters used slings and lances, weapons common to the battlefield, to fell large game. Communities delighted in the hunts because it brought a change in work patterns, as well as dancing, feasting, music, and plenty of drinking.

When nobles got together they often played *aylloscas* for high stakes. The rules for playing *aylloscas* have been lost over time. However, *cronistas* recount stories where winners acquired new lands, homes, or even young concubines from the losers.

Children played with tops, balls, and a type of dice made from bits of pottery. Girls may have had simple dolls, although it is likely that care of younger siblings replaced playing house. Children, like their parents, had little playtime and many responsibilities, including helping in the fields, harvesting crops, preparing food, and keeping their homes clean. Among the more pleasant tasks for children might have been scouring forests and meadows for medicinal herbs.

Music

Musicians were among the many artisans who lived and worked under Inca rule. Panpipes, called *sikuris* or *zampoña*, have been part of Andes music for centuries, and the haunting notes of the panpipes sang across the

Inca Music Today

Traditional music is still used to mark life events in the Andes. A house blessing or the birth of a child is a common cause for celebration, and Andes people have maintained Inca religious customs, such as planting and harvest festivals, during which music fills the thin mountain air. Community events draw pipers, drummers, and flautists to town plazas, recreating the rhythms of past Inca glory.

Several modern music groups play traditional Inca or Andes music. One of the most dramatic groups is Andes Manta. Four brothers of the Lopez family make up the quartet that plays traditional Andes folk music on more than 35 authentic Inca instruments, including the pan-pipes, *quenas*, various rattles, and drums. Andes Manta performs in Spanish and in Quechua, the language of the Incas, providing a lingering memory of ancient times long gone.

mountains and valleys of the Inca Empire. In Inca times, pipers made their own instruments from bamboo. Thin reeds (*chillis* or *icas*) produced high soprano notes, while flat, thick reeds (*toyos*) sang the bass and baritone notes.

The pipers formed a circle around their conductor, alternating notes between two or more pipers. They played the pipes by blowing across the opening at the top of each reed. Making music with pan-pipes is much like blowing across glass bottles; air moving across the hollow space creates a tone. The larger the pipes, the lower the notes and the stronger the breath required to make sound. Thus, *toyos* players needed powerful lungs.

Flutes, rattles, and drums accompanied the panpipes. Musicians made flutes (*quenas*) from bamboo and the leg bones of animals. *Quenas* range from small instruments for high notes to large ones for low notes. Their sound resembles that of a recorder. Another flute, a wooden *tarka*, provided music for religious rites and had a tone similar to an oboe.

Rattles added rhythm to Inca music. The *chác-chás* consists of a number of llama or goat hooves on a string that produce clicking noises when shaken. The *chaucha* is a natural rattle made from a dried seedpod with many small beans inside. This instrument produces a noise like Mexican maracas, and has been part of traditional Andes music since long before the Spanish arrived in Peru. Small rattles were attached to ankles or wrists of dancers, enabling them to produce their own rhythms as they moved.

Another interesting rattle is the *palo de lluvia*, which means "rain stick." To make a traditional rain stick, a musician drills holes in a long bamboo reed and slides thin sticks through the holes. Dried beans or pebbles partially fill the bamboo tube, and the ends are sealed. To play the instrument, the musician turns it upside down. The beans rattle against the sticks as they roll and produce a sound like rainfall. Like the panpipes and flutes, rattles are still used in traditional Andes music.

Drums have been around since humans first struck hollow logs with animal bones. The Andes version of the drum was made by stretching animals skins over hollow sections of wood. Military drums carried a grisly tradition: the drum skins came from the bodies of slain enemies. The pounding sound of sticks, bones, or hands against a human-skin drum instilled terror in the Incas' adversaries.

The Incas did not make metal horns, such as trumpets or bugles. However, they did use conch-shell trumpets for military, religious, and civil purposes. The military heralded the start of battle by blowing the conch. The bellow of a conch also called the faithful to temples and plazas for religious rituals. And in the civil arena, *chasquis* (postal runners) blew on the conch to alert the next post of their arrival.

Dance

Like music, dance expresses the emotions of the people. For the Inca people, dancing provided a release from work and a way to venerate their gods

Dance for Joy
Traditional dancing at the Harvest Festival in modern Cuzco preserves many of the dance forms developed by the Incas.

and actively participate in rituals. Traditional Inca dances told stories in the same way that some ballets do today. It also allowed unmarried men to pursue a potential bride, commemorate a life event such as a new child or a death, and have some fun.

Today, more than 700 dances exist from pre-Inca and empire times. These dances usually involve many dancers, some for men alone, others just for women, and still others for couples. One popular dance form, called *harawi*, originated with Inca poetry, and is really a long, sad song about lost or unrequited love and loneliness. More engaging is the *huayno*, a dance that was introduced long before the Spanish arrived in South America. The *huayno*, performed at major festivals, features couples dancing to a pounding rhythm, moving together yet rarely touching.

Today's popular folk dances in the Andes blend the traditional dances of Inca times with modern rhythms. Dance continues to be an important part of festivals and celebrations. The instruments and dance steps of Inca days blend with electric guitars and African rhythms to create the new music of the Andes.

Legends and Plays

While Inca music and dance have been preserved, the culture's literary heritage has nearly faded into oblivion. Plays, legends, and poems were passed down by oral tradition. When the Spanish arrived, they disapproved of Inca legends that claimed human rulers were gods, and would not allow myths or plays with Inca religious symbols or topics to be performed at public functions. Longer plays and myths were lost because they were never performed and could not be remembered. Thus, the few remaining bits of Inca literature are poetry and short legends—material that was easy to recite in homes.

Even the greatest chroniclers of Inca history found only a few samples of Inca literature. Garcilaso de la Vega recorded several short poems, translating them into Spanish for his reading audience.

Amautas (wise men) devised clever comedies and tragedies that were performed for the sapa inca and his courtiers. Garcilaso de la Vega claimed, "The actors were not yokels, but Incas or nobles, *curacas*, captains, and even camp commanders: each one, in fact, being obliged to possess in real life the quality, or occupy the function, of the role he interpreted. The themes of the tragedies were always taken from history, and usually related the triumphs and valorous acts of one of the early kings, or some other hero of the empire."

Sadly, the great majority of these historical dramas vanished from the Inca literary heritage once the Spanish clergy became powerful in Peru. They deemed such entertainment as pagan or heretical, since many mentioned Inca gods or referred to sapa incas as gods. Under strict Catholic doctrine, there was no place for these beliefs, and performing the plays at festivals were forbidden. Without written manuscripts, the plays quickly became vague memories.

Medicine

The herbs collected by women and children formed the basis of Inca medicine. Herbal healing during Inca times was very much like it is today. Few Andes villages have doctors or access to regular medical care, so understanding the healing properties of natural herbs is imperative for good health. In Inca times experienced medical personnel consisted of old women knowledgeable about the use of herbs, and doctors who knew how to staunch bleeding, amputate limbs on battlefields, and heal illness. A group of wandering healers, called *collahuayas*, who came from Lake Titicaca, were so skilled that they treated the royal family.

Inca medicine evolved separately from European and Far Eastern medicine, yet Inca healers pursued two medical procedures that were common in Europe and the Orient: bloodletting and trepanning. Inca *cronista* Garcilaso de la Vega describes bloodletting, which probably killed many people: "[The Incas] considered bleeding and purges to be beneficial. They bled both arms and legs, not from the vein that was probably to be effective in the case of this or that illness, but from one that seemed to them to be nearest the point of the patient's suffering. When they had a headache, they bled their foreheads, at the spot where the eyebrows

The Rainbow

In *Black Rainbow*, author John Bierhorst presents selected myths and legends of the Andes that have survived to this day. The following excerpt explains the creation of a rainbow, a powerful symbol in Inca times and a common source of interest to today's Andean people.

When the sun comes up and a mist is in the air and the whole sky is brilliant, then from a natural fountain the rainbow is born, stretching forth in an enormous arc.

But it fears the people on earth; their faces are much too lively, and it draws itself back through the sky like a braided rope of many colors.

There were once some little boys who set out to find its feet. But its toes are made of crystal and it always hides them. So the little boys were unable to find what they were looking for and they threw stones at the rainbow.

When the rainbow enters the body of a man or woman, then the person becomes gravely ill. But the sick person will be cured if he unravels a ball of yarn made of seven colors.

Herbal Remedies Prevail

Herbal remedies in Inca times reduced fevers and coughs, healed broken bones, and stopped itching from insect or animal bites. The same herbs perform the same functions in today's Andes.

Matecclu, a wetland plant with a single leaf on a narrow stem, provides effective treatment for eye infections. Corn, one of the staples of the Inca diet, helps prevent the accumulation of kidney and bladder stones. Applications of a concoction made from *chilca* leaves relieves aches from rheumatism, while sarsaparilla, a soft drink ingredient, relieves painful sores. Of course, coca, which held a pri-

mary place in the Inca pharmacopoeia, is still used to treat altitude sickness, relieve hunger, and battle fatigue. The *molle* tree provides berries for making beer, bark to improve the healing of open wounds, and twigs that make excellent rudimentary toothbrushes.

Herbalists in modern Peru sell their remedies at the open market. Along with the package of herbs, patients can get a quick diagnosis and instructions on using the compound. Many of the primary ingredients used in these medicines are the same as those used in today's prescription drugs, including quinine and coca.

meet. Their lancet was made of a silex blade, fastened in the fork of a small, split stick, the tip of which they placed over the vein, they struck the other end of the stick with a flick of the finger."

Trepanning—cutting holes into the skull for medical purposes—was common practice on the battlefields where men struck by stone clubs often had crushed skulls. Often, coca and other drugs were used to numb the patient before surgery began. Relieving pressure on the brain from such wounds or removing bone splinters were not the only reasons for trepanning. Mental conditions (schizophrenia and bipolar disorders) and physical afflictions (epilepsy and migraine headaches) may have been other reasons for brain surgery.

It appears that peoples of the Andes performed brain surgery on living patients earlier in history and more often than other world cultures. Archaeologists have dated trepanned skulls back to roughly 400 B.C.E. Literally hundreds of skulls with a variety of circular or rectangular holes cut into them have been found in burial mounds throughout Peru—many more than exist from other civilizations that performed trepanning. Scientists discovered through forensic medicine that, in some cultures, trepanning was performed on corpses as a way to release the spirit or soul of the deceased. Inca incisions, on the other hand, were performed on living bone. Examination of Inca trepanned skulls reveals that bone healed, and a surprising number of the patients lived.

Healing involved the entire community. Women assumed responsibility for care and feeding of the sick, and this included anyone within the *ayllu*. Since people rarely lived alone, someone was always on hand to tend a wounded or sick person. Itinerant healers consulted with local herbal experts in choosing the correct prescription for any ailment. The Inca culture left nothing to chance, however, and also used supernatural forces to aid the healing process. Ritual sacrifice, such as burning coca leaves or cloth, encouraged the interest of the appropriate gods.

Although people of the Andes cultures did not experience disease of epidemic proportions—smallpox, measles, or flu—before the arrival of the Spanish, they did contract serious ailments. Evidence indicates that tuberculosis, malaria, syphilis, and leprosy existed in the Andes during Inca times, as well as intestinal and stomach worms, such as tapeworms and pinworms, and lice infestations.

The lack of a written language handicapped the advance of Inca medicine. Knowledge of how to diagnose and treat disease had to be handed from parent to child, and many potions were no doubt lost. Luckily, Spanish priests preserved many recipes for herbal tonics, infusions, and ointments when they recorded local remedies in their journals.

Mathematics and Science

As with medicine, Inca science and mathematics did not advance much during the years of the empire because no written language existed. Discoveries resulting from experimentation were often lost because people with scientific interest could not write down the processes or conclusions they derived from their efforts—which also would have enabled them to share these discoveries more widely with others.

Geologic events (earthquakes and volcanic eruptions) and catastrophic weather patterns (droughts or blizzards) were, to the Inca mind, the result of angry gods. The people attempted to mollify the gods' anger by sacrificing food, cloth, and, occasionally, humans to stop the catastrophe.

Astronomy, a subject that captivated Mayan and Egyptian minds, generated limited Inca interest. People observed the movements of the sun, moon, and the planet Venus. They also recognized the shift in the sun's path that accompanied the winter and summer solstices. In Cuzco, Inca architects built eight towers, four facing the rising sun and four facing the setting sun. The towers were set so that the sun's path could be traced and noted. On the solstices, the sun left no shadow beside key columns.

Eclipses caused great furor in the Inca Empire. Garcilaso de la Vega described the attitude of the Inca toward solar and lunar eclipses:

> For them, when the Sun was in an eclipse, some misdemeanor committed in the kingdom had irritated it, since, at that moment, its countenance had the disturbed look of a man in anger, and they predicted, as astrologists do, the imminence of some severe chastisement. During an eclipse of the Moon . . . they said it was ill, and that if it continued in this state, it would die and fall down to earth; that it would crush them all under the weight of its body, and that this event would be the end of the world. At this thought, they were seized with such fright that they began to play on horns and trumpets, timpani and drums . . . they would tie up their dogs both large and small, and beat them hard to make them bark and bay at the Moon . . . they thought, if the Moon heard them baying for her, she would awaken from the dream in which illness held her a prisoner.

Botany and zoology also held little interest, except as they helped to increase crops or raise healthy llama herds. Through botanical experimentation, the Incas developed new varieties of potatoes and corn that produced more or larger vegetables, greater resistance to frost or cold, or increased production in arid regions.

Mathematics in the Inca world related to practical applications derived by empirical means. Again, the Incas had no written numerical system, so theoretical mathematics never developed. However, mathematical calculations enabled the Incas to survey and portion out acreage among the ayllus. *Quipus*, the Inca knot database, recorded crop and manufacturing yields, assessed taxes, and recorded payments. In addition to the *quipu*, the Incas developed a counting board, a *yupana*, which today's mathematicians believe was used in the same way as a Chinese abacus.

The Incas relied heavily on their version of the decimal system. Groups of 10 were important to the civil government and within the military. The basic unit of civil management was the *ayllu*, a group of 10 households. Similarly, the basic unit in the military was a troop of 10 soldiers. From there, Inca management developed larger elements with a leader for each level. A *curaca* never managed a group of 1,046 households, since unwieldy amounts were unacceptable. Instead, the "extra" 46 households were folded into a new precinct, realigning perhaps dozens of communities to establish precise units.

When the Spanish arrived in the Inca Empire, they were astounded by the accuracy of the Inca census. The civil authorities knew how many people lived in the empire, as well as their age, sex, marital status, profession, social class, productivity, and location. With advanced technology and supercomputers available to the United States government today, a national census is taken every 10 years and the resulting statistics allow for error rates of varying percentiles. The Incas developed enough government bureaucracy to redo their census, reapportion agricultural plots, and reassess taxes every year.

Building and Architecture

Inca architects and engineers had the greatest understanding of and use for practical mathematics. They produced accurate scale models of buildings, towns, and local topography. They understood elevations, angles, and how terrain affected building plans. Of all the legacies left by the Incas, surely their architectural achievements are the most enduring.

The Inca army marched along paved roads that stretched from the empire's northern extremity to its southern border. The roads, mostly paved with stone, connected region to region, city to city, with all roads eventually leading to Cuzco. The roads followed two basic systems: the Andes system, built along the mountain passes and valleys; and the coastal system, running along the Pacific Ocean. Each terrain presented obstacles. The mountains were steep, treacherous, and rugged, while the coastal roads passed through dry desert with its blowing sands. East-west roads connected the north-south highways and made travel to any region easy. At its greatest, the empire maintained more than 15,625 miles of roads.

The roads were the principal transportation routes for government officials, battalions of soldiers, and shipments of food and goods (mostly tax payments). Every few miles along the roads, rest areas provided shelter, food, and clothing for travelers. These rest areas were supported by the sapa inca and maintained by government workers.

Enduring Symbols
These standing monuments are in the ruins of Tiahuanaco, an Inca building in Bolivia. The well-fitted stones in the wall in the background are a testament to the skill of Inca masons.

105

Transportation hubs, called *tampu*, existed at key crossroads and were equipped with huge lodges for housing dozens of travelers or the military. Huts along the Inca roads housed *chasquis*, the Inca equivalent of a postal service.

Mountainous terrain has an abundance of seemingly impassable ravines and fast-flowing rivers. Inca engineers devised several styles of bridges to traverse them. Engineers favored felled tree trunks as bridges over narrow streams or crevasses, and they built stone bridges by laying slabs across a gap.

However, true Inca ingenuity came with the *huaros, uruyas,* and *tarabitas*, which resembled modern-day cable cars. Thick willow branches were interwoven to create baskets or gondolas, which were suspended from hemp ropes of strong *chawar* fiber. The ropes, fastened to tree trunks or boulders, were strong enough to support one or two people in each gondola. Once the Spanish arrived, they transported their horses across ravines using harnesses hooked over the ropes. Says Carmen Bernand in *The Incas: People of the Sun*, "Whereas in the valleys river crossings were made by raft, the mountain torrents were crossed using rope bridges or baskets suspended from cables. Moreover, all these crossing points were supervised, and nobody could carry a load across without paying toll."

Suspension bridges of corded leather, hemp rope and agave fiber were called "braided bridges," and were remarkably strong and durable. A bridge of this sort spans the Apurimac River near the present-day town of Qheswachaka.

Extensive building programs required millions of hours of labor, which were provided mainly through the *mit'a*. Every *puric* contributed a few weeks each year to the government, during which he was assigned to whatever project was the local priority. *Mit'a* projects built and maintained roads, bridges, government buildings, irrigation ditches and canals, and temples. Hundreds of skilled masons, architects, and engineers kept busy throughout the year, contributing the knowledge needed to oversee every project.

Of great interest to today's architects was the Inca use of geometric shapes in building. Trapezoids (four-sided figures in which only two sides are parallel) were used as doorways, windows, alcoves, and niches. The broad end of the trapezoid served as part of the foundation, and the narrow end supported the walls above much as a lintel supports a doorway. The northeast wall of Inca Roca's palace, built in the 14th century, is an

Machu Picchu

The mountaintop retreat of Machu Picchu (in Quechua the name means "old peak") remained hidden in the Andes for centuries, until Hiram Bingham, a Yale University professor, found the site in 1911. In truth, the ruins were never "lost," since local people always knew exactly where Machu Picchu was—at the top of a 9,000-foot mountain.

The site contains a remarkable city that was once a royal estate—a country palace—for the sapa inca. Shrouded by mountain mists are more than 150 houses, temples, baths, storage rooms, and palaces. The site has a cemetery, facilities for processing grain, and a plaza for festivals. One of the most remarkably beautiful features of Machu Picchu is the abundance of fountains, which were created from natural springs that ripple down rock walls or pool in sunken tubs.

The stonework stands as a testament to the skills of Inca masons. Walls are built of cut stones that are fitted so tightly that a knife will not pass between them. Some of the building stones weigh more than 50 tons.

Artifacts found at Machu Picchu include vessels of bronze, copper, and silver, ceramic plates and bowls, bracelets, pins, earrings, and tools, such as knives and axes. There was no gold. Since it was a country estate, the elite left their valuable possessions at the end of their stay, rather than abandoning the site as the result of an emergency. Also, there were no royal burials at the site, although scientists have found the skeletal remains of about 174 individuals at Machu Picchu.

The local people were careful never to reveal the location of Machu Picchu to the Spanish. The conquistadors eagerly looted temples and sacred *huacas*, while Catholic priests destroyed any idols and altars they found. Today, Machu Picchu is a United Nations World Heritage site and a major tourist attraction for people willing to hike along the top of the Andes Mountains.

Earthquake-Proof Masonry

In light of the damage done by earthquakes in recent years, architects might well consider applying techniques used by the Incas to join stone to stone. The basic materials of Inca stonework were simple: locally available limestone or granite, elementary stone tools, water, and sand.

An architect developed a plan for a building, complete with a scale model. Skilled masons and builders marked out the preliminary foundation according to the model. Then came the clever work—fitting stone to stone.

Stones were cut at the quarry and moved to the building site by brute force, because the Incas did not have wheels or pulleys to lessen the burden of shifting stones weighing many tons. While it is impossible to know with any certainty, some scientists believe the Incas used levers to hoist the stones onto small spherical stones, like cobblestones, that served as "casters" that enabled the workers to move multi-ton stones. The stones were then sorted by size and shape, fitting the pieces together much like a jigsaw puzzle. At that point, a skilled mason shaped two adjacent stones with matching concave and convex junctures. This technique is known as scribing and coping, and resembles the modern cabinetmaker's technique called dovetailing.

Says author John Hemming in *Monuments of the Incas*, "There was no secret formula, no magic chemical that could shape the stones, nothing but cutting with stone axes, abrasion with sand and water, and the skill and dedication of Inca masons." Primitive techniques, perhaps, but the fit between stones was so tight that many of these walls remain standing today, such as the funerary buildings at Wilcawain in northern Peru, which were built nearly 1,000 years ago. They have outlasted Spanish architecture and modern construction projects in a region plagued by earthquakes. Applying the Inca concept of joining building materials together might well be an inexpensive way to reduce damage in earthquake-prone countries.

excellent example of the Inca use of polygonal blocks. Some blocks in this palace are 12-sided, yet each stone links with its neighbors in the typical interlocking fashion. The elements at Machu Picchu were carved at the site from local material. Most doors and windows were made of multiple blocks.

The Inca civilization emphasized functionality over beauty, practicality over whimsy in every area—except for the use of water. Architects and engineers showed a surprisingly fanciful bent when incorporating springs and streams into their work. Wherever possible, the flow of water was altered so that natural springs bubbled up into decorative pools or streams gushed from stone spouts. In palaces, water spilled out of stone pipes into large pools, then cascaded into smaller basins and exited along open aqueducts.

While many examples of Inca architecture remain, historians believe that more would have survived if the Spanish had not been so determined to eradicate all remnants of non-Christian religion. Unquestionably, the most accomplished construction went into producing temples, which the Spanish either dismantled or built over whenever possible. The walls of the Coricancha in Cuzco, for example, became the foundation stones for the Spanish-built Church of Santo Domingo, and the Catholic church in Huaitará rises atop a marvelous Inca temple adorned with trapezoidal windows and niches.

Epilogue

IN A SMALL TOWN IN THE ANDES, A MOTHER RISES BEFORE dawn. She blows on the dying embers in the hearth, encouraging the fire to rekindle. She picks up a bucket and goes to a nearby stream for fresh water. Returning to her one-room adobe hut, she prepares a breakfast of hot corn meal and potatoes.

Her husband and two oldest sons rise and clear away their pallets of hand-woven blankets. After eating, they join several men and head toward one of the community potato fields, an hour's walk from the village. The men carry hoes, shovels, and empty sacks; it is time to harvest potatoes, a backbreaking job that will last for days.

At home, the mother wakes her three youngest children. They eat breakfast as she prepares a lunch of potato soup and *chicha*. Her daughters help her feed the chickens and guinea pigs, milk their one cow, and clean the house. Cleaning takes little time since the family owns no furniture other than a plain wooden stool. Dawn breaks as she heads to the fields with *almuerzo*, the hot lunch needed to fortify the workers.

During the afternoon, the mother prepares dinner for the workers and families. She slaughters, skins, and roasts guinea pigs. Her daughters prepare another dish featuring the ubiquitous potato and two dozen ears of corn. Of course, *chicha* will slake the workers' thirst. She wraps the dinner in a blanket and carries the food and beer to the fields on her back. There, she spreads out the feast and everyone shares the meal.

The family returns to their home to sleep before beginning yet another day digging potatoes from the hard Andes soil. Subsistence farming remains the economic model for *campesinos*, the people who scrape by in the mountains of Peru and Ecuador.

OPPOSITE
Still Welcoming the Sun
Thousands of people gather at the ruins of Machu Picchu to celebrate the Festival of the Sun–an Inca rite that has been revived in many communities.

111

This family scene differs only slightly from peasant life in Inca days. The food, home, and method of making a living remain the same. The clothes are slightly different, although most people still wear material they or their neighbors make themselves. Many outlying towns have no electricity or running water; some have no school for the children to attend, and most children work to help their families survive.

The spirit of the *ayllu* continues in present-day Andes communities. Neighbors and family plow, plant, and harvest together. They share in crops, preparing and storing food, and building or repairing homes. As in Inca times, citizens maintain roads and irrigation canals, and every family must provide this service or pay a heavy fine.

The community or several neighboring villages support regular local open markets. At these markets, cloth, hats, leather goods, herbs, surplus produce, and foods, such as roasted corn on the cob and grilled llama meat, are sold. Interested buyers haggle over prices, paying in either currency or by bartering their own goods. The markets provide an opportunity for people to exchange goods and gossip.

The main difference between ancient and modern times is the radio. At night, once darkness descends, the family lies on their pallets and listens as Peru's national team takes on Brazil in soccer.

Casting Off the Spanish Yoke

The Inca Empire was once a vast, sprawling dominion, stretching across the boundaries of several modern nations: Peru, Ecuador, Chile, Colombia, and Bolivia. Peru and Ecuador have the strongest links to the ancient empire, while only small portions of the other three countries came under Inca control. Since the dissolution of the Inca Empire, the five countries have shared several common conditions: unstable governments, wars, poverty, threats to natural resources, and human rights struggles for indigenous people.

From the 16th century to the 19th centuries, Spain ruled former Inca lands with total disregard for the welfare of Native peoples. The 1800s brought a resurgence of national pride and the struggle for independence among the citizens of the former Inca Empire. Peru declared its independence in 1821, although complete liberation did not come until 1826, after Simón Bolívar (1783–1830) led the people in a revolution. Bolivia ousted the Spanish in 1824, after a rebel victory led by General Antonio José de Sucre. The new Bolivian government (named after Bolívar) struggled under the leadership of corrupt politicians. In 1836, Bolivia allied itself with Peru, forming a two-country confederation. A little more than 40 later, this union was dissolved after the War of the Pacific (1879–1884), which forced Peru to cede land to Chile.

A similar revolution freed Colombia from Spanish rule in 1819 and Ecuador in 1822. Ecuador, Colombia, and Venezuela formed the Federación de Gran Colombia. Charismatic military leader Bolívar helped establish the federation. Venezuela and Ecuador left the union in 1830 to form independent countries. In 1885, Colombia formed a republic, but political differences among the leaders led to the first of several civil wars. The first civil war (1899–1902) resulted in the deaths of nearly 100,000 citizens; the second (1949–1957) left behind a devastated country awash in blood.

Chile's independence came as Spain fell to an army led by José de San Martín (1778–1850) in 1817. The country's new leader, Bernardo O'Higgins (1778–1842), established a government that slowly replaced dictatorship with democracy over many years. The third party in the War of the Pacific, Chile acquired copper-rich territory from Peru and Bolivia at the war's end.

Still Hard Work
Despite ongoing political upheaval, life for the rural people of Peru changes very little. A man on Amantani Island in Lake Titicaca carries handmade bricks on his back.

The 20th Century

The 20th century brought more chaos to former Inca territory. Peru's quest for democracy waned as a string of dictators took over the government. Between 1968 and 1980, Peru came under control of a military junta. While it was not democratically elected, the military regime did carry out extensive land reform. Radical groups arose, such as Shining Path (*Sendero Luminoso*) and the Tupac Amaru Revolutionary Movement, that waged guerrilla warfare against the military government. When representative government was restored, these groups targeted the democratically elected regimes of Fernando Belaunde, Alan Garcia, and Alberto Fujimori (a descendant of Japanese immigrants) with brutal attacks that have had far-reaching negative consequences for the civilian population, especially in rural areas.

Modern Bolivian politics consists of a series of wars and military coups. The country embarked on a war with Paraguay in the 1930s that lost territory for Bolivia. A radical miner's political faction, the National Revolutionary Movement, seized power in 1943 and again in 1952. While attempts to reform mining and land use failed, the Bolivian people demanded change. In 1964, guerrilla leader Ernesto "Che" Guevara (1928-1967) led a military coup to overthrow the government. Guevara was a communist who fostered a people's revolution in Bolivia. Communism did not produce positive results in Bolivia, and Guevara was killed in a Bolivian jungle in 1967. Guevara's government was followed by a series of oppressive military governments.

Ecuador's politics over the past century mirrored the military coups and dictatorships of its neighbors. Radical student groups rioted in the streets in 1987, the economy failed, and yet, new military dictators replaced the old ones—and nothing changed. Continued political unrest, particularly among indigenous peoples, forced the removal of the most recent president—Jamil Mahaud—in 2000. Mahaud's successor faces continued economic problems.

Colombia's government remains filled with corruption and undermined by powerful drug lords who dominate the country, its military, and its police. During the 1980s, political murders became daily events as drug cartels funded rebel guerrilla factions and highly paid assassins. In the 1990s, radical military groups, such as the Revolutionary Armed Forces of Colombia (FARC) and the National Liberation Army (ELN), terrorized the country, blew up oil pipelines, and kidnapped wealthy businessmen.

Chile's population fared no better in their political leaders. Socialist leader Salvador Allende (1908-1973) the elected president of Chile in the 1970s, tried to establish land reform and nationalize industries. A military coup, backed by the United States, ousted Allende, and General Augusto Pinochet (b.1915) took over. Unemployment rose under Pinochet, as did

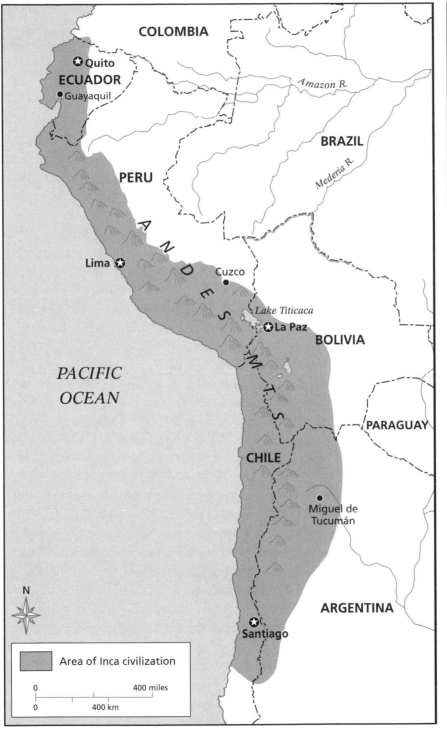

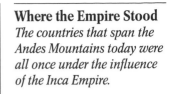

Where the Empire Stood
The countries that span the Andes Mountains today were all once under the influence of the Inca Empire.

union strikes and human rights atrocities. Government police arrested and killed many of the opposition's leaders. Chilean voters insisted on a presidential election in 1989. Pinochet agreed and lost. He remained at the head of Chile's army until 1998.

The Empire Today

Traces of Inca greatness and Spanish heritage mingle throughout the five nations that once formed the Inca Empire. Nearly half (45 percent) of Peru's population consists of Quechua people, called *indígenas*, while mestizos (people of mixed Quechua and European heritage) make up another 37 percent. Spanish and Quechua are official Peruvian languages, and many *indígenas* speak only Quechua, the Inca tongue.

Most of the people who today live in the territory of the former Inca Empire follow the Roman Catholic faith. Spanish missions and churches successfully converted the society, and nearly 90 percent of the population belongs to a local parish. However, the dominance of Catholicism does not mean that the ancient gods and religious traditions have been completely forgotten. For example, Inti Raymi, the celebration honoring the sun god Inti, has been revived in some Andes communities.

Textile cooperatives in Ecuador and Peru cling to the ancient traditions of weaving and spinning, while providing indigenous peoples with supplementary incomes. Among the most affluent weavers' cooperatives are those at Otavalo and Taquile. Otavalo weavers ply their textiles at a market in Quito, Ecuador. They produce tapestries, cloth, belts, blankets, and other cloth goods using either the traditional backstrap looms of their Inca ancestors or larger treadle looms, similar to those brought to Ecuador by the Spanish. A treadle loom has wooden frames and a foot pedal, or treadle. The weaver presses the treadle to separate alternating vertical threads on the loom. The weaver then slides a shuttle carrying the weft, or horizontal, thread between the warp (vertical) threads. Another step on the treadle shifts the warp threads again and locks the weft thread in place. Taquile, an island in Peru, has been home to a colony of weavers for centuries.

The colors and designs of Taquile textiles tell whether a man is married or single, or reveal social status. A knitted cap with white tufts shows a man is available; red peaks on a cap indicate he is married. Taquile belt designs depict seasonal or calendar events, such as the month for repairing roofs or planting crops.

Major Peruvian cities, such as Lima, Cuzco, and Arequipa, have become financial centers where industry, mining, and banking dominate. Yet the economy of the Inca region struggles and many of those who live in poverty are descendants of Inca subjects. Peru is in a financial crisis, with 50 percent of the population living below the poverty line. Young *indígenas* leave their Andes villages to find work in the cities, but unemployment rates of 9 percent defeat many would-be employees. They find themselves living in shantytowns on the outskirts of the cities in conditions far worse than their home villages.

The economies of Ecuador and Colombia depend heavily on agriculture; they produce bananas, coca, and coffee for export, along with subsistence foods such as corn and potatoes. Nearly 70 percent of Ecuador's citizens live in poverty, unemployment exceeds 14 percent and inflation approaches 22 percent. More than 55 percent of Colombia's citizens live in poverty, while a handful of Colombians rank among the wealthiest people in the world. Colombian unemployment has soared to 17 percent, far higher than most other South American countries; inflation is somewhat under control, at just under 8 percent.

Bolivia is the poorest country in South America. The economy depended on tin, accounting for nearly one-third of all exports, and the worldwide drop in tin prices led to a collapse of the Bolivian economy in October 1985. The loss of tin mining as a moneymaker has led to a rise in illegal coca farming. Today, coca and cocaine production accounts for half of the nation's exports and is a major problem for a government determined to eradicate coca from the economy. As in Ecuador, poverty strikes 7 out of 10 people in Bolivia. Consumer prices rise at a low 2 percent, yet most citizens are too poor to buy even the most modest necessities.

Chile's citizens fare better than their neighbors. Chileans earn more per person than most other South Americans, roughly $10,000 per person a year. Industry and service jobs comprise three-fourths of the jobs filled by the Chilean labor force. Although unemployment hovers at 10 percent, inflation is low and consumer goods are readily available.

CONNECTIONS >>>>>>>>>>>>

Tourism and the Inca Heritage

Archaeological digs and world heritage sites in the Inca region provide the people with a profitable business: tourism. Machu Picchu, Tihuanaco, Chavín Huantar, and Chan Chan draw history buffs interested in learning about the Inca culture. UNESCO lists these places as World Patrimony Sites that are preserved by local and federal agencies. Hiking the Inca Trail, the remains of the ancient Inca mountain road, while demanding, draws thousands of visitors yearly.

Conservation and environmental issues concern Andes residents, many of whom live attuned to the natural world. In Peru, uncontacted cultures (tribes that have no contact with the outside world) face invasion by loggers determined to illegally collect mahogany from protected lands. These lands belong to the tribes who live on them, such as the Amahuacas,

Raising the Dead

In 2002, archaeologists used bulldozers to exhume thousands of Inca mummies buried under a ghetto on the outskirts of Lima, Peru. The bodies, roughly 500 years old, included at least 2,000 men, women and children, although scientists estimate that the graveyard may contain more than 10,000 dead.

Mummy bundles—groups buried together— held up to seven corpses, binding children and parents together for eternity. Says David Braun in "Thousands of Inca Mummies Raised From their Graves": "About 40 of the mummy bundles are topped with false heads, known to archaeologists as *falsas cabezas*. Such heads, some covered with wigs, were known to be attached to mummy bundles that encased members of the Inca elite. Until this discovery, only one *falsa cabeza* from the Inca period is believed to have been documented. Also recovered were 50,000 to 60,000 artifacts, from personal valuables to food and everyday utensils."

The discovery provides archaeologists and historians with evidence of how the Inca people lived, their burial rites, and beliefs. The evidence is considered very reliable, since the mummy bundles lay undisturbed by grave robbers. The mummies were preserved under ideal conditions, and hair and skin remain intact.

The graveyard lay under a shantytown named Tupac Amaru after the last Inca ruler. It provided a refuge for Andes residents who left the mountains during the 1980s to escape guerrilla factions.

An archaeologist cleans a skull found at an Inca graveyard that dates from between 1100 and 1400.

the Shanamahuas, and the Yora Yaminaguas, and the tribes have met the arrival of logging teams with bows and arrows. They also string thick vines across rivers to prevent access to their land by boats. Although the harvest of mahogany in this region is illegal, poached wood can yield the thieves millions of dollars each year.

Pollution from mining operations, air pollution in cities, deforestation, and water pollution are some of environmental problems faced by peoples of the region today. In Ecuador, Peru, and northern Chile, arid deserts are engulfing oases and river verges, as the Atacama Desert expands. Desertification adds to soil erosion and reduces productivity in villages where subsistence farming remains the mainstay of the people. Environmental problems derive from sprawling cities, industrialization, and increased population, and affect all citizens. Each of the countries has developed federal conservation plans; their success remains to be seen.

After 800 years, the basic structures that once supported the Inca Empire survive. Shadows of roads, agricultural terraces, and irrigation ditches carve their patterns across the land. Remnants of architecture, artistry, and religion endure despite efforts to erase them from history. Quechua, the language of the people, flows in modern conversations. The Inca lifestyle and commitment to community living continues in Quechua families. The Inca work ethic flourishes in the warp and weft of backstrap looms, their shuttles carrying homespun yarns to produce textiles of remarkable beauty that are a living legacy of their ancestors.

Time Line

C. 1200	Manco Capac and Mama Ocllo found the Inca Empire and the city of Cuzco.
1228–1258	Sinchi Roca, Manco Capac's heir, builds agricultural terraces and drains the local march near Cuzco, ensuring an adequate food supply for the growing empire.
1258–1288	Lloque Yupanqui improves the Intihuasi and builds the Acllahuasi, creates public markets, begins building the extensive Inca road system, and establishes the Inca administrative system.
1288–1318	Mayta Capac establishes a school system among Inca nobility, encourages religious tolerance, and conquers the people of Tiahuanaco, a culture of superb builders and masons.
1318–1348	Capac Yupanqui rebuilds the Intihuasi and Acllahuasi and extends the empire westward to the Pacific Ocean.
1348–1378	Inca Roca reorganizes the Inca political and social structure.
1438–1471	Cusi Yupanqui defeats the Chanca and proclaims himself sapa inca, taking the name Pachacuti. He rebuilds Cuzco. He and his son and grandson greatly expand the empire.
1493–1525	Huayna Capac extends the empire into present-day Ecuador and Colombia, and declares Quito a second capital.
1525	Huayna Capac dies of smallpox. Civil war divides the empire.
1532	Francisco Pizarro, the Spanish conquistador, captures Atahuallpa.
1533	Atahuallpa is tried and executed by the Spanish.
1535	The Spanish install Manco Inca as a puppet leader of the empire. Pizarro's younger brother, Gonzalo, takes charge in Cuzco, sparking an Inca rebellion. Manco Inca flees.
1544	Manco Inca is assassinated by followers of Diego de Almagro, Pizarro's estranged business partner.
1572	The Spanish execute Tupac Amaru I, the last true sapa inca. The last outpost of the Inca Empire, Vilcabamba, falls into ruin.
1911	Archaeologist Hiram Bingham rediscovers the hidden city of Machu Picchu.
2002	Thousands of Inca mummies are discovered outside Lima, Peru.

RESOURCES: Books

Bernand, Carmen. *The Incas: People of the Sun* (Harry N. Abrams, Inc., 1993)

> A well-organized presentation of everything Inca—food, clothing, history, economy, and conquest—including material from a number of primary sources, collected at the back of the book.

de Betanzos, Juan, translation by Roland Hamilton and Dana Buchanan. *Suma y narracíon de los Incas* (Narrative of the Incas) (University of Texas Press, 1996)

> Possibly the most readily available primary source document about the Incas, their history, customs, and daily lives. Juan de Betanzos was a government clerk who observed Inca life firsthand and compiled his observations into this book.

Malpass, Michael. *Daily Life in the Inca Empire* (Greenwood Publishing, 1996)

> Malpass explains in detail how the Incas lived, worked, prayed, and expanded their culture.

Thomson, Hugh. *The White Rock: An Exploration of the Inca Heartland* (The Overlook Press, 2003)

> This is the ideal book for people who would like to trek the Inca Trail through the Andes but do not have the money or energy. Thomson describes his own adventures in the Andes in vivid detail.

Wood, Michael. *Conquistador* (University of California Press, 2000)

> Wood brings takes a more sophisticated, culturally sensitive look at the conquistadors students learn about in elementary school. Appropriate to the Inca Empire is the chapter on Francisco Pizarro.

RESOURCES: Web Sites

Descendants of the Incas
www.incas.org
> The web site of The Center for Traditional Textiles of Cuzco will give you a flavor of the rich culture of Inca people living today near the city of Cuzco, once the capital of the Inca Empire.

4 2 explore: Incas
www.42explore.com/inca.htm
> This is a well-organized page of links to other sites that discuss specific aspects of Inca culture, from agriculture and farming to food and religion, to its influence in Peru today and the Incas' relationship with the conquistadors. It includes a whole section on Inca mummies.

Ice Mummies of the Inca
www.pbs.org/wgbh/nova/peru/
> In September 1996, archaeologist Johan Reinhard led an expedition to the summit of Sara Sara in Peru in search of frozen sacrificial mummies. Reinhard's expedition was filmed by the BBC is and documented on this web site as a NOVA/PBS Online Adventure. Here you'll find daily accounts and images from the expedition, e-mail questions and the responses from the team, and much more.

Inca Civilization
www.crystalinks.com/incan.html
> An overview of Inca civilization, including science and the arts, with lots of great pictures and maps.

The Incas Art and Culture
www.theincas.com
> This comprehensive web site presents Inca history, gold work, pottery, masonry, and other aspects of Inca culture. Lots of pictures illustrate every aspect of the site.

Incas and Conquistadors
www.hc09.dial.pipex.com/incas/
> A complete presentation of the Incas, how they were conquered by the Spanish, Inca ruins, and the Spanish who ruled Peru.

The Life, Times, and Execution of the Last Inca
www.jqjacobs.net/andes/tupac_amaru.html
> A narration of Tupac Amaru's last years and how he tried to regenerate the greatness of the Inca Empire.

The Living Edens: Manu
www.pbs.org/edens/manu/
> A presentation of the remarkable people, animals, and plants that inhabit Manu Rainforest Preserve in Peru.

Pre-Colombian History in South America
http://berclo.net/page94/94en-hist-sam-pc.html
> An in-depth explanation of the cultures that preceded the Inca Empire, and what the Inca learned from them.

The Sacred Hymns of Pachacutec [Pachacuti]
www.red-coral.net./Pach.html
> One of the rare examples of Inca literature appears on this site. These hymns of Pachacuti, translated into English, were composed for the Situa ceremony around 1440 to 1450.

BIBLIOGRAPHY

Ascher, Marcia, and Robert Ascher, *Mathematics of the Incas: Code of the Quipu*. Mineola, N.Y.: Dover Publications, 1981.

Bernand, Carmen, *The Incas: People of the Sun*. New York: Harry N. Abrams, 1993.

de Betanzos, Juan, *Narrative of the Incas (Suma y narracíon de los Incas)*. Translated by Roland Hamilton and Dana Buchanan. Austin, Tex.: University of Texas Press, 1996.

Bierhorst, John, *Black Rainbow*. New York: Farrar, Strauss and Giroux, 1976.

Braun, David, "Thousands of Inca Mummies Raised From Their Graves," National Geographic News. URL: news.nationalgeographic.com/news/2002/04/0410_020417_incamummics. Updated April 22, 2002.

Burger, Richard L. and Lucy C. Salazar, Ed., *Machu Picchu: Unveiling the Mystery of the Incas*. New Haven, Conn.: Yale University Press, 2004.

Callañaupa, Nilda, "A Message from Nilda Callañaupa," Descendants of the Incas. URL: www.incas.org. Posted 2001.

Chuchiak IV, John F., Lecture #29, "Colonial Responses to the Bourbon Reforms: Discontent and Indian Rebellions in the Viceroyalities of Peru & New Spain (1748–1800)." URL: http://history.smsu.edu/jchuchiak/. Updated December 2003 (Accessed April 23, 2003).

de Cieza de León, Pedro, *Chronicle of Peru* (The Second Part of the Chronicle of Peru). Translated by Clements R. Markham. London: Hakluyt Society, 1883.

Cobo, Father Bernabé, *The History of the New World*. Translated by Roland Hamilton. Austin, Tex.: University of Texas Press, 1983.

Guaman Poma de Ayala, Felipe, *La nueva crónica y buen gobierno*. Biblioteca Ayacucho, 1980.

Hemming, John, *Monuments of the Incas*. Boston: Little, Brown and Company, 1982.

Jacobs, James Q., "Tupac Amaru, The Life, Times and Execution of the Last Inca." URL: www.jqjacobs.net/andes/tupac_amaru.html. Posted 1998.

James, Peter, and Nick Thorpe, *Ancient Inventions*. New York: Ballantine Books, 1994.

Karen, Ruth, *Kingdom of the Sun*. New York: Four Winds Press, 1975.

Malpass, Michael, *Daily Life in the Inca Empire*. Westport, Conn.: Greenwood Publishing, 1996.

Marrin, Albert, I*nca and Spaniard: Pizarro and the Conquest of Peru*. New York: Macmillan Publishing Company, 1989.

de Molina, Cristóbal, *The Fables and Rites of the Incas*. Madrid, Spain: Historia 16, 1989.

"Palacio de la Conquista," The University of New Mexico Conexiones. URL: http://www.unm.edu/~conspain/trujillo/. Updated 2003.

Pizarro, Pedro, *Relation of the Discovery and Conquest of the Kingdoms of Peru*. Translated by Philip Ainsworth Means. New York: Cortes Society, 1921.

Sarmiento De Gamboa, Pedro, *History of the Incas*. Mineola, N.Y.: Dover Publications, 1999.

Stierlin, Henri, *Art of the Incas*. New York: Rizzoli International Publications, 1984.

Editors of Time Life Books, *Incas: Lords of Gold and Glory*. New York: Time Life Books, 1992.

"Tupac Amaru II," Incaita. URL: www.fortunecity.com/millennium/lilac/3/tupac.htm. Updated 2001.

Urton, Gary, *Inca Myths*. Austin, Tex.: University of Texas Press, 1999.

de la Vega, Garcilaso, *The Incas: The Royal Commentaries of the Inca Garcilaso de la Vega*. Translated by Maria Jolas from the critical, annotated edition of Alain Gheerbrant. New York: The Orion Press, 1961.

de Xeres, Francisco, *The Conquest of Peru (1534)*. Translated by Clements R. Markham. London: Hakluyt Society, 1970.

Zuidema, Reiner Tom, *Inca Civilization in Cuzco*. Austin, Tex.: University of Texas Press, 1990.

INDEX

Page numbers followed by *i* indicate illustrations, page numbers followed by *m* indicate maps.